TEXTURE EFFECTS
FOR RUBBER STAMPING

NANCY CURRY

NORTH LIGHT BOOKS
CINCINNATI, OHIO
www.artistsnetwork.com

ABOUT THE AUTHOR

2

Nancy Curry is a freelance artist and project designer who teaches mixed media techniques, rubber stamping, bookmaking and paper arts at stores and larger paper arts venues around the country. Nancy's work often varies applications of media resulting in pieces with richly textured surfaces that alternately intrigue and inspire her audience.

Nancy's technique-rich classes are based on her own journey of discovery. They stress the importance of play as a necessary tool to restore the creative spirit, confidence and joy in one's artistic life. Seeing the "I can do this" moment in her students' eyes is her renewal.

Nancy's current menu of play includes altered book collaborations, mixed media paper weaving, and calendar art journaling. Her resumé of published work includes *Somerset Studio*, *Stamping Arts and Crafts*, cover art and special features in *Rubber Stamper*, *Expression*, *Vamp Stamp News*, *Belle Armoire*, and work in an art textbook for Harcourt School Publishers. Nancy resides in Mason, Ohio, with her husband Jim, daughter Sammi, and studio dog Bogart.

Visit her websites:
www.picturetrail.com/nancycurry
www.picturetrail.com/ncurry (altered books)

"Art is not what you see, but what you make others see."—Edgar Degas

08 07 06 05   5 4 3

Library of Congress Cataloging-in-Publication Data

Curry, Nancy
Texture effects for rubber stamping / Nancy Curry
 p. cm.
Includes index
ISBN 1-58180-558-6
1. Rubber stamp printing. 2. Texture (Art) I. Title

TT867.C87 2004
761--dc22
2004043369

Editor: Tonia Davenport
Designer: Leigh Ann Lentz
Layout Artist: Kathy Gardner
Production Coordinator: Sara Dumford
Photographers: Christine Polomsky and Tim Grondin
Photo Stylist: Nora Martini

METRIC CONVERSION CHART

TO CONVERT	TO	MULTIPLY BY
Inches	Centimeters	2.54
Centimeters	Inches	0.4
Feet	Centimeters	30.5
Centimeters	Feet	0.03
Yards	Meters	0.9
Meters	Yards	1.1
Sq. Inches	Sq. Centimeters	6.45
Sq. Centimeters	Sq. Inches	0.16
Sq. Feet	Sq. Meters	0.09
Sq. Meters	Sq. Feet	10.8
Sq. Yards	Sq. Meters	0.8
Sq. Meters	Sq. Yards	1.2
Pounds	Kilograms	0.45
Kilograms	Pounds	2.2
Ounces	Grams	28.4
Grams	Ounces	0.04

DEDICATION

For my daughter Samantha:

I am who I am today because you are here. Thanks for being patient during my chance to dance. I hope when you get the chance, you will dance, too.

ACKNOWLEDGMENTS

Special thanks go to:

My husband Jim, whose constant support, love and belief in me has helped me grow in different directions. I couldn't imagine not being able to share all this with you.

North Light's awesome staff, especially Tricia Waddell, who gave me the chance to share my art; my editors Liz Schneiders, Christine Doyle and Tonia Davenport who kept me calm, organized and centered as I learned the process and Christine Polomsky, photographer extraordinaire.

My friends, family and peers who have been an integral part of my art journey, especially this new path I am on.

MaryJo and PJ who taught me to play, and my friends who have played with me. Special hugs for Charla and Tracy who were happy to lend an ear and counsel while I went through this new author process. Their encouragement and support always keeps me grounded and I treasure our connection.

My home stores Stamp and Art Specialties, Stamp Your Art Out, and other stores I've visited that went all out to make me feel welcome. My students, I am so grateful for the encouragement and the amount of inspiration they have provided.

Finally, my mother, whose spirit gave me the courage to go into a new direction in my life. When I was growing up, she always told me I could do anything I set my mind to and finally, I listened.

TABLE OF CONTENTS

IRRESISTIBLE ELEGANCE

TACTILE & TEXTURAL TACTICS

SPOT COLORATION

SURFACE ALTERATION

WATER PLAY

TEXTURAL MUSINGS

■ ■ ■ ■

I have always been fascinated by what lies beneath the surface in people, life and art, so it is not a surprise that my art focus has been on design techniques that combine visual and physical textures. The projects and gallery pieces in this book will appeal to stamp artists wanting to add textural mixed media elements to their paper arts and beyond. The visual textures used invite the viewer inside the layers, while the physical or tactile elements guide the viewer's eyes around the piece or act as a finishing focal point. These easy-to-follow techniques use a wide variety of materials that will allow the stamp artist to create artwork that has visual depth and sophistication, yet will work with any style or experience level. The artist's own personality, along with their knowledge and choice of materials will make the artwork unique, while serving as a launching point for a new creative journey.

Many of my techniques in this book were born through play. Sitting down without any design pressure is a freeing process. Explore these products and methods, and then add some of each that you are familiar with. Some combinations will meet with success, while others won't. Whatever the results may be, you will channel the knowledge that comes from discovery, into your future projects. Most of all, find enjoyment in your journey.

"Creativity exists more in the searching than in the finding."
— Stephen Nachmanovic

MATERIALS

I've found that this art hobby is part process and part collection. What you'll find on these next pages are tools and materials that I have collected and have developed preferences for. On your journey you have probably developed your own likes and dislikes. Don't throw those out for these, but rather pick and choose what works for you now and play.

Tools of the Trade

Having the right tools makes the project flow smoothly so that you can have fun with the art. The collection doesn't happen overnight, so you might need to make some substitutions while building your repertoire.

Heating Tool

For power and ease of control, the Milwaukee is my favorite. For heat setting and working with shrink plastic, I move the nozzle farther away to slow the process down. Always keep the nozzle moving to prevent burning or damage, and never apply heat to a cutting mat because it will warp it. Try heating on a ceramic tile, a block of wood, a Teflon-coated sheet, or, if using powders, a box lid.

Cutting Tools

I usually use a craft knife and cutting mat when working on my pieces. Change your craft knife blade often and avoid pushing down too hard while cutting. Let the blade do the work and just be a firm guide. A good, self-healing cutting mat is a must as well. For repetitive or precision work, invest in a good paper cutter.

Rulers

I prefer the High-Vis clear ruler from JudiKins for its steel edge and tinted markings that can be seen on light or dark paper. The Centering Ruler by Creative Imaginations is also great to have for spacing embellishments, brads, etc.

Bone Folders

These are wonderful scoring tools that provide seamless paper creasing. They also work well for burnishing.

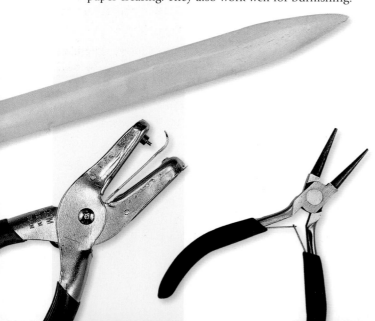

Hole Punches

Standard-sized hole punches are essential. Available in many shapes, they are great for embellishments, cutouts and borders. A Japanese hole punch is a great tool to have. It allows for the placement of a hole anywhere on the surface and it works on many types of surfaces.

Stamps

Have a variety of rubber stamps available when you begin projects. Look for quality stamps that are trimmed closely (or trim them yourself with a craft knife to prevent ink spillover) and etched cleanly. I recommend cleaning your stamps before the first use to remove any manufacturing residue.

Scrap Papers

When creating, you'll want to have scrap paper on hand to protect your work surface. Deli or waxy palette paper is a great surface for items that might stick. I generally use old magazines or pads of newsprint for other stamping needs.

Brayers and Squeegees

Brayers come in many sizes and types. They are great for rolling out ink and paint over larger surfaces. I also like to use them dry when stamping larger detailed stamps onto difficult surfaces like acetate or laminate. Textured or removable-head brayers are great to add patterns or "noise" to artwork.

Old credit cards, plastic paint scrapers and the Dove rubber squeegee are all great tools with which to spread and remove paint, inks and glues.

Pliers

Wrapping and coiling wire is faster and easier with round-nosed pliers. They do not pinch or nick the wire in places as some other tools do, and you get a smooth flow of the wire throughout.

Applicators

There are many ways to apply paint and inks to papers. Standard and compact-sized stipple brushes as well as Color Dusters are great for textural ink or paint addition. I enjoy the convenience and disposability of non-latex cosmetic sponges, and I use them daily in my studio to apply paints and inks. The use of a felt applicator is a very practical way to apply alcohol inks to your projects.

Spray Misters

These bottles are great for misting water, and other liquids used for cleaning, adding texture or sealing. I keep a few spares in my studio for thin mixtures of paint as well.

Paper and Other Surfaces

It is good for a studio to have a mixture of both heavy and light weight cardstock, in a variety of textures and colors, as well as an interesting assortment of handmade and specialty papers. Blank index cards in varying sizes are also good to have on hand for a quick layer on a card. Be sure to stock posterboard, vellums, shirt box tissue and mulberry paper as well. Office supply stores are a great source for manila tags in various sizes. If you're like me, you'll find collecting paper to be addictive.

Laminate and Acetate

Cold laminate sheets can be found at office supply stores or through various stamp companies. I prefer the heavyweight variety for my uses. Acetate is found at office supply stores near the overhead projection supplies. JudiKins sells embossable window plastic that withstands heat without warping.

Shrink Plastic

Lucky Squirrel's PolyShrink delivers the most even shrinking I have found. I work primarily with the translucent, but black, white and clear varieties are available, too.

Papier-Mâché

Papier-mâché comes in many different shapes and sizes for holiday and decorative functions.

Glues and Adhesives

Glue preference will vary with what you are used to using and what you are trying to attach. Read the labels to make the best choices for your surfaces.

Fluid Adhesive

My favorite way to attach fiber and wire is with Perfect Paper Adhesive. I use a liner paintbrush and paint the glue where I want the fibers or wire attached. After adhering my elements, I weight the area with a heavy stamp until dry. The glue will be virtually invisible on your projects and it is archival.

Dimentional Adhesive

This is a glossy adhesive I like to use for beads, mica or other uneven surface embellishments. It is also a great medium to mix with paints or dyes. Diamond Glaze is my preferred choice.

Industrial Adhesive

I use this type to attach heavier components for a secure hold such as tile to tile placement, shrink plastic, and button attachments. For smaller areas, I apply with a toothpick. Be sure to use it in a well ventilated area. E6000 works the best for me.

Tapes

I use good quality double-sided liner tape on many of my paper projects. For a secure fit, I generally tape the top, sides, and bottom edges, as well as the middle. The projects in this book were done with Incredi-Tape, but there are several brands that will be safe and archival for your artwork.

I love the wide rolls of JudiKins Eclipse Tape for masking because I can cut or tear what I need and don't have to spend a lot of time piecing.

I use Scotch Vellum Tape to adhere lighter-weight papers like vellum and mulberry that otherwise would show the heavier liner tapes or glue.

Hardware store variety masking tape is a great ink applicator. You can't beat the price and ease of use.

Hot Glue

A hot glue gun is in my studio more for embellishment play than it is as an adhesive. I like the thicker glue sticks because they go further.

Pigments, Paints and Inks

These all come in different varieties. Knowing their properties will help you choose the correct ones for your projects, but have fun and experiment.

Dye Inks
Dye inks are water-based and quick drying on glossy or matte cardstock. My favorites are the Adirondacks by Ranger because of the rich and varied color palette. I use both the pads and re-inkers and seal them to help reduce fading.

Pigment Inks
Pigment inks are thick, opaque and slow-drying. They work well on all types of paper, but most must be embossed or heat-set on glossy surfaces. They are also fade-resistant.

Chalk Inks
I prefer the ColorBox Fluid Chalks by Clearsnap because of their juicy pads, color choices and layering possibilities. Be sure to heat set these for permanence.

Metallic and Pearlescent Inks
I love the colors in the Brilliance and Encore Ultimate Metallics lines from Tsukineko. The Brilliance will dry on its own or heat sets well to permanence on vellum, acetate, mica and even shrink plastic. The Encore Metallics are best used on matte cardstock, but can be sprayed to seal on other surfaces.

Permanent Inks
StazOn by Tsukineko is my favorite solvent-based permanent ink that is designed for both porous and semi-porous surfaces. I use it on paper, glass, shrink plastic, acetate, dominoes and clay with wonderful results.

Resist Ink
Resist ink prevents other dye inks from changing the color of the paper beneath. Ranger Clear Resist is my favorite because of its thin, fast-drying formula. I use both the pads and re-inkers for many of my designs.

Alcohol Inks
Alcohol inks are staples in the illustrator and graphic arts market. Always have the clear blender on hand to dilute or enhance spreading properties. Solvent-based, permanent and waterproof when dry, my favorites are the Jacquard's/USArtquest's Piñata inks and the Studio II Ink*Its by Graphic Marker.

Powdered Pigments
Most of my experience has been with Jacquard's Pearl-Ex. Pearl-Ex can be mixed with various mediums for many different art functions. The interference colors will be used for projects in this book.

Acrylic Paints
The two types of acrylics used for projects in this book are Jacquard's Lumieres and Plaid Glaze Vernis. Lumiere paints are highly pigmented, light-bodied and remain opaque and bright on dark surfaces. They work well on paper, wood, canvas and fabric. Plaid Glaze Vernis is a faux finishing paint that works well for paint removal techniques. I often use these paints together. The glazes can be simulated by mixing gloss gel medium and regular acrylic paint.

Watercolors and Brushes
There are many watercolor paints available. I have developed a preference for the Dr. Ph. Martin's Hydrus watercolors and the Lyra Aquacolor crayons. I love the Hydrus for their pigment concentration and the Lyras for their variety of application. I also use tubed and Peerless watercolors. Experiment and find the ones you like best. I don't buy expensive brushes for the type of watercolor that I do; I buy different styles and sizes that are moderately priced. Foam brushes are great to use with watercolor for washes, but one brush I could not live without is the Niji Waterbrush by Yasutomo. I love the water control and portability. Try one for yourself.

Webbing Spray
Krylon Webbing Spray makes a fine web of paint on surfaces. I spray large sheets of paper and then put them away to be used as backgrounds later on.

Leafing Pens and Metallic Rub-Ons
The best way I have found to achieve a gilded look on any surface is with the Krylon Leafing Pen. It comes in metallic gold, silver and copper and provides great permanent coverage.

Metallic Rub-Ons by Craf-T Products can be used on cardstock, glossy paper, clay, wood or canvas, and as an accent, highlight or a full, opaque colorant. Apply with fingers or cotton applicator, and seal if necessary to finish.

Finishing Touches

Interesting embellishments can be pulled from other art hobbies, or purchased at hardware and decorating stores. The sky's the limit, or rather, your imagination is. Here is a list of some of my favorites:

Wire

Wire can be used as a finishing focal element or to pull the eye around the perimeter of the card. It should be secured well to withstand a lot of handling. I prefer using 20-24 gauge wire for most of my projects.

Fibers

Fibers come in many types and can be used in many different ways, such as making tassels or attaching tags, incorporated into a flat design to form regions, or gathered under other embellishments. They can be found in many craft, needlework, knitting and art stores. Or look for old sweaters begging to be unraveled and recycled into art.

Embossing powder

Add texture to a repetitive design by using clear embossing powder. The design will be repeated, but the clear motif will not take up visual space.

Other Add-Ons

Brads and eyelets are a great way to secure layers, but I also love to incorporate them as a visual element to my designs. Use them to accent an area of interest.

Buttons easily add interest and physical texture to paper arts, boxes and canvas projects. Shanks can be removed easily with a button shank remover, so they lie flat.

Beads of all kinds are just fun to use to liven up a composition. Try the small, holeless variety for lumping or making clusters, small seed beads for borders or adding texture to a design and larger beads for fibers.

Mica tiles come in many sizes and a few different colors. I like to use smaller pieces as focal embellishments with my art. They work well as the support for glue seals and fibers and are easily gilded or tinted.

Add some pizzazz to glue seals or to a background with any type of glitter glue.

Sealants

After all of my hard work, I like to protect my finished work with a sealant. Krylon Matte Finish spray is my sealant of choice on paper arts projects. For protecting decorative tiles, I use Future Floor Finish, followed by polyurethane.

TEXTURE TOOLBOX

Have these items available for all projects in this book.

- scrap paper
- scissors
- stamp cleaner
- double-sided tape
- heat tool
- cutting mat/craft knife
- ruler
- bone folder
- cosmetic sponges
- matte finish spray

BASIC TECHNIQUES

Making a Felt Applicator

I use inch-sized (2.5cm) wooden cubes or spools, inexpensive felt squares and the hook half of a hook and loop fastener to make the applicators. Alcohol inks are then applied to the felt.

Applying Straight Alcohol Ink

Alcohol ink is evaporative by nature, so it dries very fast on many surfaces. Apply it in a pouncing, circular motion, as I did here, when a spreading effect is desired. Apply in a linear motion to tint larger areas.

Alcohol Inks with Clear Blender

Apply two to three drops of green alcohol ink to a clean piece of felt on your wooden cube. Add a drop of clear blender to the felt and pounce. The blender will dilute and spread the color, resulting in different color values.

Mix Different Shades and Blender

Place a drop or two of two or three different colors and a drop of clear blender on a clean piece of felt and pounce. The blender will mingle with the colors and new colors will result.

Using Spray Webbing

Spray the webbing slightly past the paper onto scrap so the webbing falls onto the paper in a random pattern. Always hold the can three to four feet (.9m to 1.2m) away from the paper.

Inking a Brayer

Roll the brayer over a stamp pad in one direction. Lift and place it back on your starting point on the pad. Roll again in the same direction. Repeat until the roller is fully inked.

Stamp Cleaning 101

The Ranger Rub-It Scrub-It pad fits perfectly in an 8" × 8" (20.3cm x 20.3cm) aluminum foil cake pan, and has become the cornerstone of my cleaning system. I wet down the pad with water and spritz with diluted window cleaner. Rubbing the stamp on the mesh pad will eventually clean all water-based inks and paints. When working with solvent-based inks, I first rub the stamp with JudiKins Permanent Ink Cleaner and then scrub in the pad to finish. I tap the stamp onto a wet paper towel to remove the solvent residue and let dry.

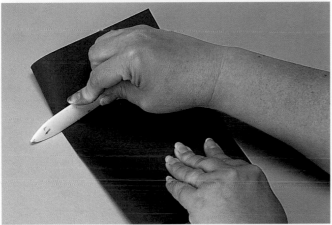

Fold from the Middle

To get crisp folds, it is better to score along a line and then fold. If there is a time crunch, I skip the scoring and line up the edges. Then I crease the center of the fold with the point of the bone folder and use the flat portion to pull from the center to the edges of the card.

Play with Mounting Options

I have learned to play with multiple mounting options before making my final choice. Different color choice in papers and mounting styles will affect the mood of the finished artwork. I pick out four or five choices to start: colors pulled out of the centerpiece work, complements to the color scheme used, white, and black. Then I begin shuffling them around to see what works with my vision. It does sometimes take more than one sitting to mount my work, but much of it is finished with this procedure. In the instance here, a black mounting layer adds a touch of drama to the finished design.

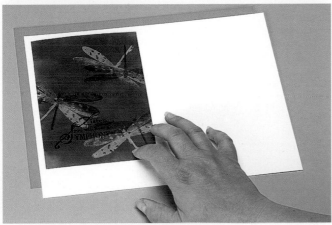

Vary High-Contrast Paper Choice

White is a high-contrast mounting option to consider. Often I will add it as a narrow layer between several other layers.

IRRESISTIBLE
ELEGANCE

This chapter is aptly named as I do find myself unable to resist these techniques time and time again. Old becomes new as I try different color mixes, design options or finishing techniques. New tools and materials come into the limelight to keep the possibilities fresh and interesting, while some old favorites come back into favor as well. Resist gets better and better with more play and allows me to create pieces that are not only rich in composition but also personalized to my unique style.

I have taught these techniques for several years and have found that they showcase everyone's unique style. Once classes are turned loose to begin making backgrounds, I often find it hard to get them to want to stop to mount or finish, instead choosing to continue playing with color and pattern. Their enthusiasm is contagious. I often find that my studio time mimics their experiences, as there are days I just want to stain and play, saving piles of untrimmed papers that will later be turned into finished art. I love having that pile in reserve because many of the pieces require only minimal mounting to become elegant, finished cards. So, I do let myself have a resist day every so often to keep my cupboards full. Be sure to save pieces that you aren't jazzed about. Often they can be punched, cut or combined with embellishments to be given new life.

Let these projects take your own creativity in a new direction as you rediscover color play. I hope you will find the process irresistible, too.

DRAGONFLY SONG

I like to use resist backgrounds to create different moods. Using two to three colors that are close together on the color wheel creates a subtle blend of light and shadow. Brighter colors by their nature mean more movement and suggest a light mood, while darker colors can be used to create more drama or sophistication. These projects both feature dragonflies, but I chose different color palettes and mountings to give each its own identity.

■ ■ ■ ■ MATERIALS LIST

- glossy white, white and mauve cardstock
- clear resist ink pad
- black permanent ink pad

- dye ink pads: Adirondacks in Caramel, Currant, Raisin, Espresso *(Ranger)*
- matte finish spray
- dragonfly stamp *(Impression Obsession)*

- phrase stamp *(Impression Obsession)*

  Finished size:
  7½" × 5½" (19.1cm × 14cm)

1 Stamp With Resist Ink

Randomly stamp the dragonfly three times with clear resist ink on glossy cardstock cut to 6½" × 4½" (16.5cm × 11.4cm). As a rule, an odd number of stamped images produces a more pleasing composition to the eye.

2 Heat to Set

Heat the resist ink for ten to fifteen seconds with a heat tool. Keep the gun in motion and four to five inches (10.2cm to 12.7cm) away to ensure that the paper dries thoroughly without scorching.

3 Start Paper Staining

Pick up some Caramel ink on the tip of a non-latex cosmetic sponge and begin staining the paper. Add Currant ink onto the same sponge and continue until the card is covered with both inks. I generally use the same sponge if the ink colors are all mid-range or darker, but feel free to use a different sponge for each color. This first layer of color should be applied with very firm pressure to ensure a bright resist. I find that using a circular motion will result in a smoother application with fewer staining lines from the sponge. A moldable ColorToolBox Stylus System tip is also an effective blender for this technique.

4 Shade to Deepen and Blend

Add a third accent color using Raisin. Apply Espresso brown to portions of cardstock to blend, shade and unify color scheme. Complementary colors can also achieve the same effect.

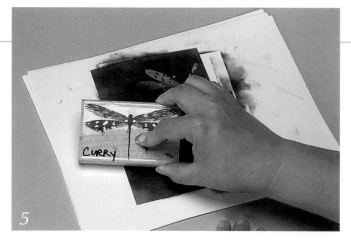

5 Overstamp to Bring Out Design

Ink the dragonfly stamp with Raisin and stamp the card, offsetting these dragonflies slightly from those in resist. Stamping the design a second time is called overstamping. Where you place the overstamped image is a matter of choice and will change the composition. Try some different placements for variety. If you are using different colors than I am, selecting a dark ink will result in a greater contrast with the resist.

6 Stamp Final Layer

Stamp phrase using black permanent ink for a high contrast final layer. A permanent ink is the best ink to use for this layer.

7 Spray to Seal

Hold can 12" (30.5cm) away and spray a light coat of matte finish spray. Repeat after one minute. Sealing this project is a matter of preference, but I prefer a satin or matte finish to create a sophisticated mood.

8 Trim and Mount

Mount resist piece onto trimmed white cardstock and then onto the mauve folded card with a good double-sided tape. I prefer double-sided tape to glue or glue sticks because of its ease of application, quick bonding, and longevity. Trim the folded card if necessary. A clear ruler makes accuracy easy.

TRADE SECRET Different brands of glossy cardstock take ink staining differently. The resist projects in this book were done with King James, but much of what will be readily available will be Kromekote. When working with Kromekote or cardstock of unknown origin, stain the entire piece with the lightest ink before continuing with other inks. This will produce the desired muted effect. Posterboard and matte coated paper can also be used for resist but the end result will be more subtle. ■

VARIATION:
IN FLIGHT

■ ■ ■ ■

MATERIALS LIST

- glossy white and yellow cardstock
- clear resist ink pad
- dye ink pads: Adirondacks in Caramel and Butterscotch *(Ranger)*; Nick Bantock in Chrome Yellow and Damson Plum *(Ranger)*
- paper adhesive
- matte finish spray
- dragonfly punch
- dragonfly stamp *(Impression Obsession)*
- splatter stamp *(Art Impressions)*

Finished Size:
6" × 6" (15.2cm × 15.2cm)

1 Stain Over Resist

Create a background paper using the same resist technique with yellows (Caramel, Butterscotch and Chrome Yellow). Shade randomly with Damson Plum and overstamp dragonfly. Stain a second piece with yellows and stamp splatter with Caramel. Seal both with matte spray.

2 Stamp to Repeat Pattern

Stamp splatter in Damson Plum on folded sheet of yellow cardstock.

3 Punch Out Embellishments

Punch out three dragonflies from the second stained paper and glue them randomly to the card's left side. Trim the dragonfly piece to fit the card, leaving about 2" (5cm) for the spine.

TUMBLING FEATHERS

I envisioned feathers blowing along the ground when I created this card. I liked the linear movement the feathers created so much that I wanted to add some excitement in the background to continue the flow. Then I remembered the bleeding tissue that was popular a few years ago, and thought that the tissue dye might make some interesting high-contrast areas. I love the energy the chunky pieces bring to the design.

■ ■ ■ ■ ■ MATERIALS LIST

- glossy white and dark teal cardstock
- art tissue in shades of blue and green
- clear resist ink pad

- dye ink pads: Adirondacks in Lettuce, Bottle, Stream, Denim *(Ranger)*
- metallic ink pads: Encore Metallics in Teal, Blue *(Tsukineko)*
- gold seed beads
- matte fluid adhesive

- matte spray finish
- spray bottle
- feather stamps *(Stamp Francisco, Stampscapes, Hero Arts, Fred Mullett, PSX)*

Finished size:
5½" × 8½" **(14cm × 21.6cm)**

1 Stamp and Dry Resist Ink

Stamp assorted feathers in a horizontal band across the center of the glossy cardstock. Vary the direction and placement of the stamps to create a freeform design. Dry thoroughly with a heat tool.

2 Tear and Place Tissue

Tear several shades of blue and green art tissue into small scraps. Randomly arrange the bits around the card, being careful to avoid the resist areas.

3 Spritz to Activate Bleeding

Holding the spray bottle a few inches from the paper and lightly spritz each tissue-covered area with water.

 TECHNIQUE TACTIC If the scraps seem to want to fly around, spray them in midair and then arrange them on the glossy cardstock. This also cuts down on the amount of water that is on the card, but note that some color will transfer to your fingers as well. ■

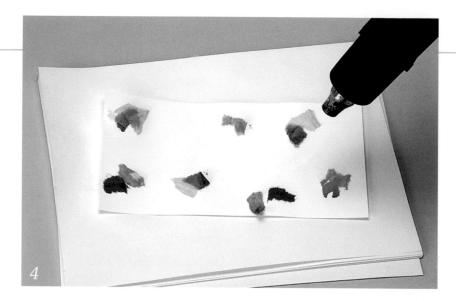

4 Dry Tissue and Peel Away

Dry with heat tool and peel away scraps. This tissue is very pigmented so the resulting colors will be vibrant. Save the scraps to be used again for a secondary bleeding. The results will be less vivid, but still will allow for contrast.

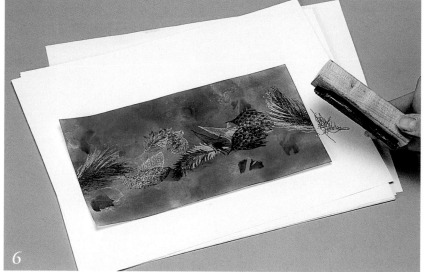

5 Stain to Reveal Resist

Using a cosmetic sponge and firm pressure, begin rubbing Lettuce ink over the entire card to reveal the resist image. Repeat with Bottle and Stream, and a couple of accents of Denim.

6 Overstamp for Detail

Overstamp the same feather stamps in Denim and Stream ink. This unifies the background color and brings back some detail that was blurred in the resist.

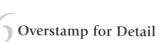

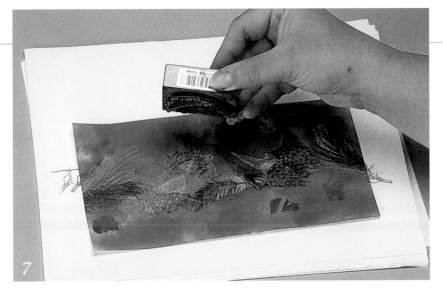

7 Add Highlights and Seal

Overstamp some feathers across the band with Blue and Teal Encore inks. These inks will add subtle highlights throughout the band, but they will not dry on glossy paper without sealing. If finish spray is not wanted, the inks could be embossed with clear embossing powder for permanence.

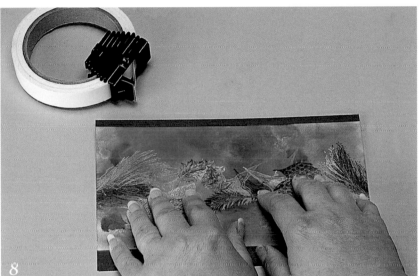

8 Mount Onto Cardstock

Mount the finished resist piece a little closer to the top, rather than the center of the teal card with double-stick tape. This will leave a weighted bottom and room for embellishments underneath.

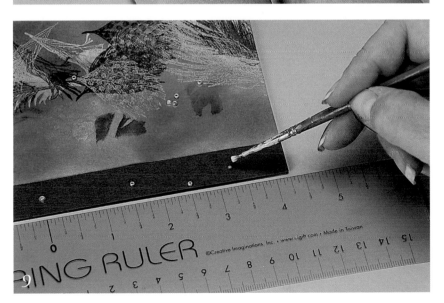

9 Embellish With Beads

With paper adhesive, glue clusters of gold seed beads onto the card to accent. Using a centering ruler, glue single seed beads to create a border along the bottom of the card.

 TRADE SECRET I use matte Perfect Paper Adhesive to glue all of my embellishments, fibers, and wire that will show, because it dries invisibly. Use a thin liner brush to dot glue where you will place an object. In the case of holeless beads add a second coat of glue to ensure a good bond. In the case of wire that typically doesn't want to stay put, place a piece of waxed paper and a heavy, wood block stamp on top until the glue sets. ∎

SILENT WHISPERS

This project is a monochromatic study in greens, that I tried during a rainy spring, but the composition can be done in any color scheme. The floral stamps complement the irregular masking and are placed in a haphazard manner to continue the line. To spark some interest and add some contrast to the background, I added metallic highlights to some of the flowers.

▪▪▪▪ MATERIALS LIST

- glossy white, purple and pale yellow cardstock
- clear resist ink pad
- black permanent ink pad

- dye ink pads: Adirondacks in Pesto and Eggplant *(Ranger)*; Nick Bantock in Sap Moss Green *(Ranger)*
- metallic ink pad: Encore Metallic in Purple *(Tsukineko)*
- art masking tape

- matte finish spray
- floral stamps *(Hero Arts)*
- phrase stamp *(Marks of Distinction)*

  Finished size:
  5½" × 7½" **(14cm × 19.1cm)**

1 Create Torn Mask and Stain

With resist ink, stamp a variety of flower stems on glossy cardstock. Dry thoroughly with a heat tool. To create an irregular edge, tear a 3" (7.6cm) wide strip of masking tape and position it a couple of inches from the right edge. Using firm pressure and a cosmetic sponge tapped into ink, begin blending shades of Pesto, Sap Moss Green, and then Eggplant for shadowing. Work from left to right continuing the process downward until the entire section is covered. Remove the masking tape

2 Repeat, Changing Ink Color

Tear another strip of tape and press it down to the left of the first. Change the angle of the tape from the first strip and press firmly. With a new cosmetic sponge and more firm pressure, stain paper with Sap Moss Green ink and a bit of Pesto by pulling the color away from the masking tape, toward the first stripe. It won't hurt the design to have the new ink run over the first stripe so no masking of finished sections is required. Repeat this process with the alternating color combinations and torn tape until the card is covered.

3 Stamp the Flowers

Apply Sap Moss Green to the stem and Eggplant to the blossom of one of the flower stamps. This two-toned effect will create a more realistic design. Stamp and repeat for the other flowers. Offset each one so they appear close to, but not directly over, the resist image. For highlights, stamp some of the blossom heads with Encore Purple Metallic.

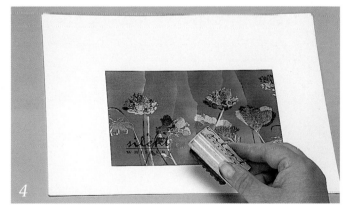

4 Add a Phrase, Seal and Mount to Finish

Stamp the phrase using black permanent ink. Seal with matte finish spray. It will take three light coats to seal the metallic completely. Mount the image onto a slightly larger piece of purple cardstock with double-sided tape. A final mounting on folded yellow cardstock acts as a frame for the vibrant center.

SAGE BARGELLO

Bargello design has its foundation in the needlework arts but transfers well into paper crafting. It is characterized by long straight lines worked into flame patterns or other geometric designs.

The linear nature of bargello inspired me to try blending it with resist to make special designs that are rich in visual texture. Sage Bargello's muted design comes from a single background stained with compatible colors, while Medley, on page 29 mixes multiple backgrounds and high contrast for a more dramatic presentation. The design options are only limited by your imagination.

■ ■ ■ ■ MATERIALS LIST

- glossy white, white and pale yellow cardstock
- clear resist ink pad
- dye ink pads: Adirondacks in Bottle, Lettuce, Pesto, Butterscotch, Caramel, Espresso *(Ranger)*

- metallic ink pad: Encore Metallic in Champagne *(Tsukineko)*
- 20-gauge gold wire
- matte fluid adhesive
- matte finish spray
- round-nose pliers

- weight, such as a large stamp
- background stamp *(Moon Rose)*
- alphabet embellishment stamp *(Moon Rose)*

Finished size:
6¾" × 5" **(17.1cm × 12.7cm)**

TEXTURE TIDBIT *The bargello effect can be achieved by collaging various related stamps or creating a resist landscape. The background will become a textural tool rather than a focal point, so don't stress too much over finding just the right stamp. I find that I've had the best results with detailed images. They seem to create the most interesting patterns for this type of segmented artwork.* ■

1 Stamp and Dry Resist Ink

Stamp the background stamp on glossy cardstock. Cover the whole surface by stamping more than once if needed. In this sample, the background was stamped twice. Dry thoroughly with a heat tool.

2 Stain to Reveal Resist

Stain entire sheet with Lettuce ink on a cosmetic sponge. Using the same sponge, gradually layer Pesto, Butterscotch and Caramel inks over the Lettuce to create a muted background. Add touches of Bottle and Espresso to shade further and unify the colors.

3 Overstamp and Seal

Overstamp, slightly offset, with Encore Champagne to create soft metallic highlights. Seal with three light coats of matte finish spray, drying between coats.

4 Cut Strips

Cut a piece of cardstock to use as a base for the strips. It will need to be 1" to 2" (2.5cm to 5cm) shorter than the length of the strips so it won't show through after completing the mounting process. This size will determine the extent of mountain and valley heights. To trim the paper into narrow strips use either a paper trimmer or a larger paper cutter. Trimming can be hand done, keeping in mind that the strips will be flush against each other so the craft knife angle must be consistent while cutting. Make the strips varying widths.

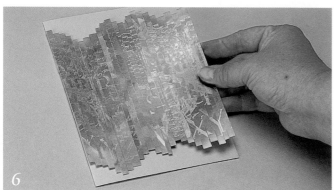

5 Mount Strips Onto Backing

Completely cover the base piece with adhesive, using adjacent widths of double-sided tape, carpet tape, or run the cardstock through a Xyron machine. Begin layering strips in the same order in which they were cut, varying the height of the strips to make mountains and valleys. Use your narrower strips at the apex of the curves for more drama and wider strips to form the gentler slopes. Continue until the design is the width of the folded cardstock.

6 Mount Bargello Design

Mount finished bargello on pale yellow cardstock using double-sided tape. Be sure to affix edges for a smooth look.

7 Stamp and Trim Embellishment

Stamp alphabet in Lettuce on a small scrap of matching cardstock and cut it into a square.

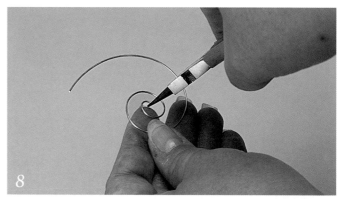

8 Coil Wire

Cut a 5" (12.7cm) piece of wire to work with. Lay the wire out to see the natural bend. Beginning at one end, coil the wire going in that direction, gradually getting looser and looser. Cut any excess wire so that the finished size of the coil is similar to the stamped square.

9 Attach Embellishments

Attach the stamped square onto the bargello card with double-sided tape. Use a thin paintbrush to draw a coil of matte fluid adhesive where the wire will rest. Place the wire on top and rinse out the brush. Use a heavy stamp to weight down the wire on the card until the glue dries.

VARIATION:
MEDLEY

■ ■ ■ ■

MATERIALS LIST

- glossy white, olive, maroon and black cardstock
- dye ink pads: Adirondacks in Cranberry, Eggplant, Denim, Butterscotch, Pesto, Caramel *(Ranger)*
- gold leaf charm
- E6000 adhesive
- matte finish spray
- music collage stamp *(PostModern Design)*
- background stamp *(Toybox)*
- flowers stamp *(Stampers Anonymous)*
- mosaic background stamp *(Stampers Anonymous)*

Finished Size:
7" × 5" (17.8cm × 12.7cm)

1 Stamp Resist and Stain Paper

Stamp and dry resist ink, using assorted backgrounds, to four small sheets of glossy cardstock. Stain each piece with different combinations of dye ink. Seal and trim into 1" × 5" (2.5cm × 12.7cm) pieces, and attach with tape to a piece of 4" × 5" (10.2cm × 12.7cm) white cardstock.

2 Cut Bargello Strips

Lay the paper so that the strips are horizontal on the cutting mat and begin cutting vertically. Be sure to keep the strips in order and vary the widths according to taste. Stagger sheets of olive, maroon and black cardstock to form the base of the card. Mount design so that it is flush with the right edge. Cut three narrow rectangles out of the same paper and tape together. Layer them onto the card with double-sided tape. Embellish further by attaching a gold leaf charm.

BAROQUE CLOCK

When making clocks a couple of years ago after much experimentation, I found that resist was my design technique of choice because it complemented the functionality of the clock without appearing too distracting. I think it works best with a layered, nondirectional motif, so often I use feathers, leaves, or more sophisticated swirls to create the design. Set it on a table easel for a very eye-catching, yet practical display.

■ ■ ■ ■ MATERIALS LIST

- glossy white cardstock
- white mulberry paper
- Plexiglas clock kit *(Magenta)*
- clear resist pad

- dye ink pad: Adirondack in Denim *(Ranger)*
- matte finish spray
- vellum tape

- Baroque flourish stamp *(Above the Mark)*
- clock stamp *(Magenta)*

Finished size:
7" × 5" (17.8cm × 12.7cm)

1 Stamp and Dry Resist Ink

On a half sheet of glossy cardstock, stamp the flourish image repeatedly to create a background design, making sure to rotate stamp angle throughout the surface of the cardstock. Dry thoroughly with a heat tool.

2 Stain to Bring Out Resist

Using firm pressure and a cosmetic sponge tapped into Denim ink, begin rubbing to bring out resist design. Even though you are working with only one color, reducing the amount of pressure will produce a lighter blue and repeating with more color in certain areas will produce darker shading. Play around with the colors until the background is filled with lights and darks.

3 Overstamp to Add Detail

Slightly offset the flourish and stamp repeatedly using Denim ink. Seal with matte finish spray to create a satin finish.

 TEXTURE TIDBIT When creating a background with a repeated motif, it's a good habit to stamp some images off the edges to prevent a "frame effect" that draws the eyes toward the borders. Compositions will then be more seamless and pleasing to the viewer. ∎

4 Trim and Prep Design for Mounting

Trim card to 6½" × 4½" (16.5cm × 11.4cm). Centering the piece on the clock, place the image face down and mark where the hole will need to be, to match up with the hole in the acrylic. Cut the hole out with a craft knife and set the card aside.

5 Begin Covering Clock Front

Cut a sheet of white mulberry paper to be 1½" (3.8cm) larger than Plexiglas support. Fold in the four corners and use vellum tape to attach.

6 Finish Front Covering

Fold in the four side flaps and affix with vellum tape.

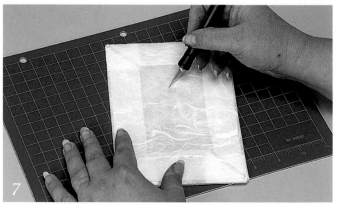

7 Cover the Back

Cut a second piece of white mulberry paper to 6½" × 4½" (16.5cm × 11.4cm) and tape it to the back of the support. Find the hole with your fingers and, using a craft knife and cutting mat, cut a hole through the two layers.

8 Mount Resist Background

Carefully match up the holes and layer the resist image over the front of the clock with double-sided tape.

9 Stamp Clock Face

Use the same resist technique to stamp, stain and seal the clock face. With a craft knife, cut a hole in the center big enough to fit over the clock shaft. Then cut around the perimeter of the clock face with scissors and attach the face onto the clock with double-sided tape. Seal with two light coats of matte finish spray.

10 Add the Clock Works

Attach the hands to the clock according to the package directions. All you need is a battery and you are all set. The clock can then be hung or placed in an easel.

TACTILE & TEXTURAL
TACTICS

I have been a tactile person throughout my life, so it is not surprising that I am drawn to art that I want to touch. This physical texture can come in the form of a focal embellishment or can be integrated into the background composition, depending on the overall project design.

Focal embellishments are attention-getters and make a statement all their own. For my work, I like the embellishment to support the theme of the piece without looking like an afterthought. However, I have seen artists create eye-catching pieces with found objects that seem unrelated, yet somehow fit. Try what will fit your style.

Texturing a background with glue or paint is a subtler approach, yet just as effective. Both work well as the sole design element or as a collaboration with fibers, beads or wire. Manipulating these materials is almost too much fun so I try to keep in mind that the textural tool used should support but not overpower the overall design. I also try to have a design plan before I begin. That usually keeps me in check.

CIRCULAR MOTION

Circular Motion is my "everything but the kitchen sink" project, but it doesn't become overdone because all the elements are unified by the repeated theme. I like the bright mood the colors convey, and to be perfectly honest, I love playing with and coloring hot glue so I plain just had fun with that. When the creative spirit isn't there, just spend some time making hot glue seals and put them away for a rainy day. Maybe they'll make you smile, too.

■ ■ ■ MATERIALS LIST

- glossy white cardstock
- clear resist ink pad
- dye ink pads: Vivid Yellow (Clearsnap); Nick Bantock in Cerulean Azure *(Ranger)*
- metallic ink pad: Brilliance in Gold *(Tsukineko)*

- alcohol inks: Piñata in Sunbright Yellow and Lime Green *(USArtQuest/Jacquard)*
- clear embossing powder
- mica tile chip
- colorful fibers
- sparkle glitter glue

- masking tape
- hot glue gun/clear hot glue sticks
- coffee filter
- spiral stamps *(Hot Potatoes and Printworks)*

Finished size:
5½" × 5½" (14cm × 14cm)

1 Stamp and Dry Resist Ink

Stamp larger spiral image repeatedly on glossy cardstock. Dry thoroughly with a heat tool.

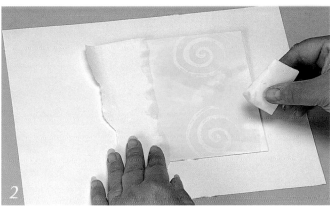

2 Mask and Stain to Bring Out Resist

Place a strip of torn masking tape vertically on the card, closer to the left side. Stain the right section of the card with the cosmetic sponge and the Vivid Yellow ink, using heavy pressure.

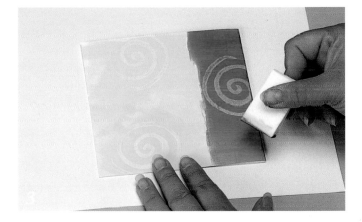

3 Remove Mask and Stain

Peel off the mask and stain the left section with Cerulean Azure using a fresh cosmetic sponge.

4 Stain the Entire Card

Continue rubbing Cerulean Azure over the entire card so that the yellow changes to green.

5 Overstamp With Both Colors

Overstamp the spiral with the blue and yellow inks, and allow to dry thoroughly before embossing.

6 Add Tactile Texture to the Background

Stamp several spirals with clear resist ink. Pour clear embossing powder over the card.

7 Tap Off Excess

Flick to tap off excess powder into a coffee filter. Use a fan paintbrush to brush off any stray powder.

8 Emboss

Heat all the powder-covered spirals until fully melted. The result will be a mixture of tactile and visual texture that will make a rich background.

9 Apply Lubricating Ink

Tap the smaller spiral stamp into gold Brilliance ink. This will act as a release agent for the stamp when it is time to remove it from the set hot glue. Any pigment ink or embossing fluid can be substituted.

10 Make a Hot Glue Seal

Squeeze a quarter-sized dollop of hot glue on a Teflon sheet or waxy palette paper. Gently lay the prepped stamp on top. Do not press down as it will naturally sink as the seal begins to set. Let the seal cool for five to ten minutes before peeling it off the stamp. If it does not want to begin to peel, it is not ready yet

11 Dye the Seal With Alcohol Ink

Apply drops of Sunbright Yellow ink outside the stamped area of the seal. Rub in with your fingers if needed. Repeat the process on the stamped area with Lime Green ink. Let both applications dry before continuing.

12 Add a Bit of Sparkle

Squeeze glitter glue into the stamped crevices of the seal.

13 Mount Embellishment

Cut two pieces of fiber and fold in half. Add a mica chip on top and glue to card with hot glue. Layer the hot glue seal on last with a small dollop of hot glue.

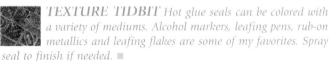

TEXTURE TIDBIT Hot glue seals can be colored with a variety of mediums. Alcohol markers, leafing pens, rub-on metallics and leafing flakes are some of my favorites. Spray seal to finish if needed. ■

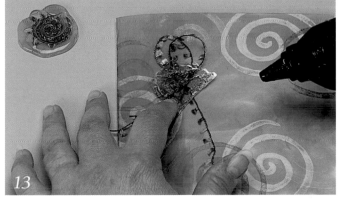

SUNSET VIEW

I've found that I like the way the mixture of paint, ink and fiber works to add texture, movement and interest to stamped projects. I think what I like best about working with these elements is the change that occurs after each layer is added. The layout is hinted at in the first layer, but as each new element is added, there is more definition that takes the piece in different directions. The metallic highlights add the final pizzazz, and the end always produces a satisfied sigh.

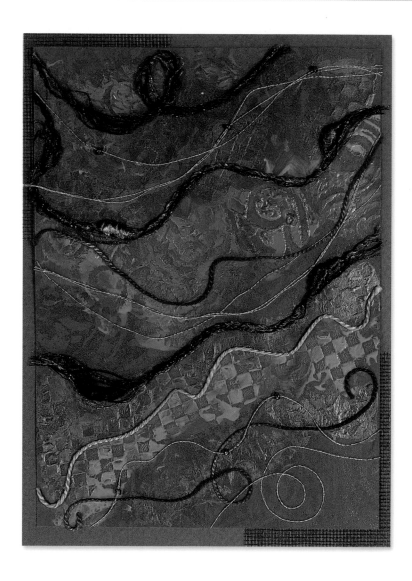

▪ ▪ ▪ MATERIALS LIST

- melon and terra cotta cardstock
- mesh paper
- dye ink pads: Adirondack in Caramel *(Ranger)*
- metallic ink pad: Brilliance in Copper *(Tsukineko)*

- acrylic paint: Glaze Vernis in Mango, Old World Bronze, Sunflower, Tangerine *(Plaid)*
- colorful fibers
- gold seed beads
- matte fluid adhesive
- Baroque stamp *(Stampers Anonymous)*

- rosette stamp *(Postmodern design)*
- harlequin mosaic stamp *(Stampers Anonymous)*
- swirl stamp *(Stampers Anonymous)*

Finished Size:
7¾" × 5½" **(19.7cm × 14cm)**

 TEXTURE TIDBIT *An effective textural effect that will appear throughout this book can be achieved by alternating the use of positive and negative application. Negative application is the removal of already applied paint with a tool or brush. Positive application means using a tool to add paint to a surface. Fuller-bodied paints (glazes, thicker acrylics, acrylics mixed with gel medium) are stiffer and stay put when partially removed to create the pattern. These techniques also work well together to build tactile and visual texture and depth at the same time.* ■

1 Stamp Design for Texture

Stamp rosette several times with Caramel ink onto melon card-stock. Overstamp with Brilliance Copper to add some metallic highlights.

2 Heat to Set

Heat set the ink with a heat tool to speed the drying time.

3 Add a Layer of Paint

Sponge a freeform wavy band of Old World Bronze glaze from left to right. The goal is to have it thick enough to pull a pattern away from it, but not too thick that the paint won't stand up after the pattern is pulled. It is a good idea to experiment on scrap to see how much paint to apply before working on a project.

4 Remove Paint to Add Texture

Begin removing paint to form the textural patterns by pressing and lifting the uninked baroque stamp in the painted area. I often use a slight jiggle to ensure that enough paint will come off. Deeply etched stamps are the best for this technique. Be sure to clean the stamp with a toothbrush or scrubbing pad in between removals so that the stamp will continue to pick up paint. Also, do not let the paints dry on the stamps.

5 Continue Building Texture

Continue the process by adding and removing Mango, Sunflower and Tangerine glazes in bands. Work one band at a time and vary the stamps for added interest. Use the paint left on the stamp to add that same pattern back in a thinner coating. Repeat over the rest of the card, and allow the paint to dry.

6 Arrange and Attach Fibers

Cut and lay out fibers along the borders of the textured bands. Vary the type of fibers used, adding beads in places. Glue each by lifting a small section at a time to paint paper adhesive on with a small paintbrush. Press down to ensure a good bond.

7 Add Mesh Before Mounting

Trim rectangles of mesh paper and mount onto the front corners of the terra cotta card. This will act as a partial frame for the finished card front.

8 Trim and Mount

When the fibers are dry, trim any excess along the edge. Center and attach the finished textured piece to the terra cotta cardstock using double-sided tape.

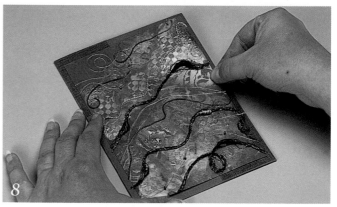

VARIATION:
TEXTURED LUGGAGE TAG

■ ■ ■ ■

MATERIALS LIST

- manila luggage tag
- acrylic paints: Glaze Vernis in Deep Woods Green, Plum and Burgundy (*Plaid*)
- assorted fibers
- mosaic stamp (*Stampers Anonymous*)

Finished size:
4¾" × 2⅜" (12.1cm × 6cm)

 TEXTURE TIDBIT *To make the tag shown on page 34, I simply cut three various sizes of shrink plastic into luggage tag shapes. I stamped and colored them before heating, then immediately after shrinking them, I molded them while they were still warm and pliable, into wavy shapes. A mesh brayer adds texture to the background, and beaded gold fibers add a touch of the exotic.* ■

1 Apply and Remove Paint

Using a cosmetic sponge, completely cover a standard manila luggage tag with a combination of glazes in Deep Woods Green, Plum and Burgundy. Create the patterned background by removing paint with the dry mosaic stamp.

2 Finish with Fibers

Add assorted fibers in varying thickness to finish.

PERFECT PAISLEY

Webbing spray is one the easiest textural tools to use once you get control of the spraying. I hadn't played with it for a couple of years so it took me a few minutes to remember that it looks better if the spray falls down to the paper. Once I got the hang of it, I sprayed quite a few sheets for later use. I'll not forget it again. Take some webbing spray of your own and have fun with it.

■ ■ ■   MATERIALS LIST

- glossy white, black and burgundy cardstock
- dye ink pads: Adirondacks in Currant, Raisin and Red Pepper *(Ranger)*; Nick Bantock in Lamp Black *(Ranger)*
- black webbing spray
- gold webbing spray
- gold buttons
- E6000 adhesive
- button shank remover
- 1½" (3.8cm) square decorative punch
- paisley stamps *(Stamp and Art Specialties)*

Finished size:
9" × 4" (22.9cm × 10.2cm)

1 Stain Cardstock

Use a cosmetic sponge to completely stain a half sheet of glossy cardstock with Currant, Raisin and Red Pepper.

2 Stamp Pattern

Stamp paisley designs randomly in Raisin and Lamp Black.

3 Spray Webbing

Spray both black and gold webbing over patterned cardstock and onto a sheet of black cardstock.

4 Punch Squares

Punch four squares out of the decorated cardstock with a 1½" (3.8cm) hole punch. If you flip the punch over, you can center the image in the cutting area for the best results.

 TECHNIQUE TACTIC When working with spray webbing, or any type of spray, use plenty of newspaper to protect your work surface and always hold the spray can 3 to 4' (.9m to 1.2m) away from the card. It works well to aim the spray slightly past the cardstock to allow the spray to fall into place. ■

5 Cut Squares Into Triangles

Using scissors (or a craft knife and cutting mat), cut triangles out of three of the four squares.

6 Mount the Pieces

Use double-sided tape to mount the triangles onto the black cardstock. Start from the top and bottom and overlap toward the center. Place the final square, turned as a diamond, in the center. Check alignment with a ruler before pressing firmly.

7 Mount Decorated Front

Mount onto the folded burgundy card, using double-sided tape.

8 Remove Button Shanks

Cut the shanks from several buttons, using a button shank remover. The flimsier the shank, the easier it will be to cut, so choose wisely.

9 Attach Buttons to Embellish

Glue the buttons onto the card front with E6000.

VARIATION:
FESTIVE

■ ■ ■ ■ ■

MATERIALS LIST

- white cardstock
- scraps of black and plum cardstock
- gold and green gel pens
- black webbing spray
- gold webbing spray
- rainbow foil
- thin gold metallic fibers
- translucent shrink plastic
- E6000 adhesive
- ⅛" (.3cm) hole punch

Finished Size:
4¼" × 4¼" (10.8cm × 10.8cm)

1 Spray Webbing

Follow the same webbing application tips and spray both black and gold webbing to the sheet of white cardstock.

2 Spot Foil

In the first few minutes that the webbing is setting, it is possible to transfer foil splotches onto the webbing for highlights. To do this, cut a small piece of rainbow foil, place it on top of a section of webbing and burnish with your fingers. Lift off quickly and continue to add highlights throughout the background. To embellish, cut a 2½" × 2¼" (6.4cm × 5.7cm) piece of shrink plastic and write "Celebrate" around the perimeter with gel pens. Cut a hole in the top center with an ⅛" (.3cm) hole punch. Shrink with a heat tool on a Teflon-coated sheet. Tie on a bow with metallic fibers and layer the embellishment onto slightly larger squares of plum and black cardstock using E6000. Center layered embellishment onto the web-sprayed cardstock to finish.

PARALLELS

I have a lot of fun playing with hot glue on paper projects. The key to having success with the glue gun is keeping your tools ready and not putting too much thought into the pattern you are creating. That will keep your linear design loose and relaxed. I also like to work this design with textured wallpaper or vellum for a change of pace. Be creative and see what you come up with.

■ ■ ■ MATERIALS LIST

- beige, dark green, and scrap card stock
- burgundy ribbed cardstock
- dye ink pads: Adirondacks in Bottle and Cranberry *(Ranger)*
- metallic ink pads: Encore Metallic in Champagne *(Tsukineko)*
- metallic rub-ons: Russet, Deep Gold, Olive *(Craf-T Products)*

- 20-gauge gold wire
- hot glue gun/glue sticks
- E6000 adhesive
- paper adhesive
- matte finish spray
- round-nosed pliers
- credit card, plastic hotel key or other scraping tool

- swirl stamp *(Paper Inspirations)*
- splotch stamp *(Art Impressions)*
- faux webbing stamp *(Just for Fun)*

Finished Size:
5½" × 5½" (14cm × 14cm)

1 Stamp a Colorful Background

Use Cranberry and Bottle ink pads to stamp the beige cardstock with splotch and faux webbing stamps.

2 Continue Making Backgrounds

Stamp the swirl stamp on burgundy and dark green cardstock using Bottle. Stamp splotches with Champagne on the green cardstock to add metallic highlights.

3 Cut and Attach Background Strips

Cut the beige and green cardstock into ¾" (1.9cm) strips and cut the burgundy into ¼" (.6cm) strips. You will need a total of three beige, four burgundy and two green strips. Alternate the beige and green strips, placing the narrow burgundy in between to border. Adhere the strips to a piece of scrap cardstock with double-sided tape. Save the excess cardstock to use for the embellishments later.

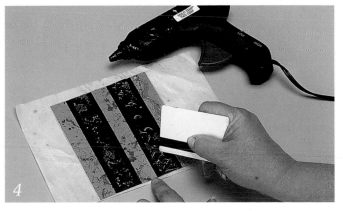

4 Texture With Hot Glue

Add hot glue in wavy lines on the beige and green bands. Texture the glue with a scraping tool by running it down the freshly squeezed glue. Working one line at a time will produce the best results. Glue and texture the leftover pieces saved in the last step as well. Allow to cool.

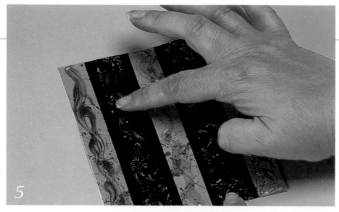

5 Color the Textured Glue

Apply Russet, Deep Gold and Olive Metallic Rub-Ons to the glue with a finger or cotton swab. Spray seal with two coats of matte finish spray.

6 Trim Borders

Trim wavy borders along the edges with scissors.

7 Mount to Card Base

Mount the wavy-cut image onto the burgundy cardstock base with double-sided tape.

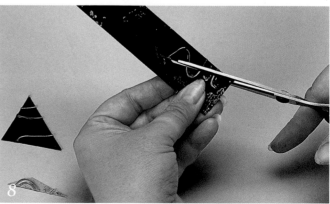

8 Cut Coordinating Triangles

Cut three triangles out of the extra textured cardstock.

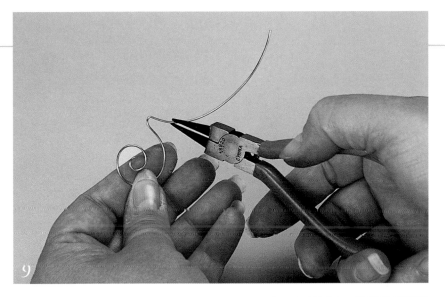

9 Make a Wire Embellishment

Cut a 5" (12.7cm) piece of 20-gauge gold wire. Coil one end of the wire about a third of the way. Crimp wire backward where the first spiral ends with round-nosed pliers.

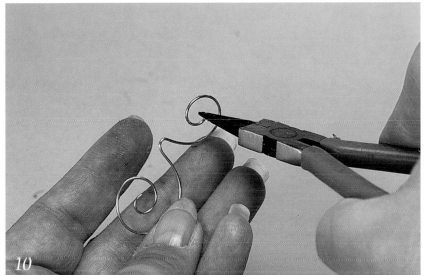

10 Add a Second Spiral

Wind another coil beginning at the other end of the wire to make a slightly smaller coil.

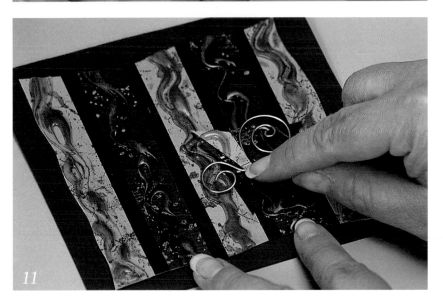

11 Attach Wire to Finish

Attach the trio of triangles onto the card with E6000. Attach the coil on top by drawing a coil of paper adhesive where the coil is to be placed. Weight the coil down to ensure a good bond while drying.

CELEBRATION

Sometimes a unique fold can make a good card look sensational. I think the folds and the closure of this piece are inviting and fun, yet the card doesn't appear juvenile and could be used for any occasion. My choice for the closure was shrink plastic, but any dimensional embellishment like a button, clay or charm could be used.

▪▪▪ MATERIALS LIST

- blue cardstock
- ¼"(.6cm) hole punch
- permanent ink pads: StazOn in Royal Purple (*Tsukineko*)
- metallic ink pads: Brilliance in Moonlight White and Galaxy Gold (*Tsukineko*)
- gold leafing pen

- translucent shrink plastic (*Lucky Squirrel*)
- gold fibers
- E6000 adhesive
- confetti stamps (*Stampassions*)
- triple diamond stamp (*Magenta*)
- small present stamp (*ZimPrints*)

- "Celebrate" stamp (*Moe Wubba*)
- "Make a Wish" stamp (*Impress*)
- "Bouquet of Dreams" stamp (*Hero Arts*)

Finished Size:
3½" × 3½" (9cm × 9cm)

1 Cut, Score and Fold Cardstock

Cut card to 3½" × 10½" (8.8cm × 26.6cm). Measure and score into thirds. Fold each side toward the center.

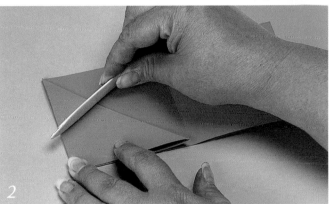

2 Fold Left Flap

Score and fold the left flap down diagonally. Flatten and crease well with a bone folder.

3 Fold Right Flap

Score and fold right flap up diagonally. Flatten with a bone folder. The two sides should meet for a crisp diagonal opening.

4 Stamp the Front

With the card closed, stamp the front randomly with presents, confetti and phrases, using Moonlight White, Galaxy Gold and Royal Purple.

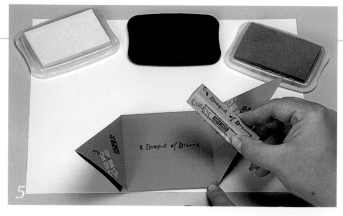

5 Stamp the Inside

Open the card and stamp the same images on the side triangles. Finish with the sentiment stamped on the center square panel.

6 Make Shrink Plastic Closure

Use Royal Purple ink to stamp the triple diamond image onto shrink plastic. Detail the image with the gold leafing pen and cut it out. Punch two holes at the center near the top with a ¼" (.6cm) hole punch.

7 Heat Shrink Plastic

Shrink the rectangle with a heat tool until flat and unmoving. While warm, flatten completely with the back of a wood stamp.

8 Add Fiber and Attach Shrink Plastic

Tie gold fibers in a bow to the shrink plastic piece and attach the piece to the bottom front flap of the card using E6000.

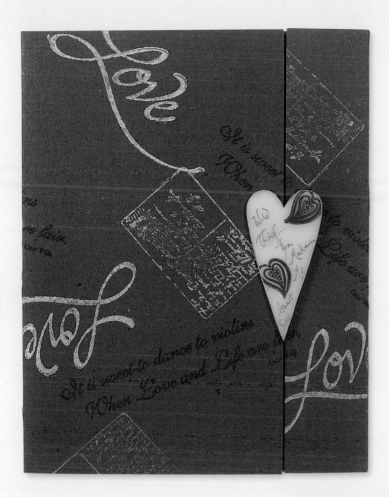

VARIATION:
LOVE

I like to experiment with different folds and closures. This card places an extra fold along the right border of the card. Cut a primitive-shaped heart out of shrink plastic, stamp it in colors that would coordinate with the cardstock, and shrink it with a heat tool. While it cools, stamp words and phrases onto the card in all directions using matte and metallic ink. This provided a background for the shrink plastic closure. Add gold leafing to the edges of the closure and attach it along one side of the fold. This was a Valentine that my husband really loved.

VARIATION:
PRETTY IN PINK

I decided to try some handmade paper for this folding technique and was very pleased with the results. Wet-tear the paper to create a feathered edge, then stamp and emboss with bronze and copper powder. For the fancy closure, shrink a piece of foam tray (like the kind meat comes on) and cover it in Lumiere and wrap it in wire. Add large beads to support the closure dimension and add interest to the card. This would work well for any occasion.

SPOT
COLORATION

We'll be using different forms of spot coloration to create contrast in the artwork presented in this chapter. These techniques will project more movement and will be more dramatic in nature, yet the elements will still be unified.

I love the use of alcohol inks to spot color on slick surfaces. The lack of control while the inks are spreading is very freeing once you get over the old "coloring book mentality." Coloring outside the lines on acetate, tile, dominoes and glass has become one of my favorite guilty pleasures. I can see my old art teachers shaking their heads.

Pull up your shirtsleeves and dive into marbling with convenient materials and a sense of fun. There is more control in this technique, but it is still exciting to watch the designs develop. I love the richness in texture that marbling brings to my cards and bookmaking. It can stand alone as a focal element or be used to support stamping. And better yet, it is a technique with infinite design and color patterns that can grow with your art as you dabble in other paper arts projects.

Thinking outside the box leads to new paths. Turn yourself loose on those paths and let yourself go wild!

TULIPA

There is something enticing and very challenging about working with acetate. I like the clarity of the images that seem to be brought to life by spot coloration, as well as the depth that comes from pale mounting. I played around with some cardstock to soften the browns, ending up with peach pastel. Don't settle on the first backing you find that works well with the spot coloration. Experiment with some contrasts or exploit an insignificant color. You'll be surprised at the different looks you can get.

■ ■ ■ ■ ■ MATERIALS LIST

- peach and cream cardstock
- acetate
- black permanent ink pad
- alcohol inks: Piñata in Burro, Havana Brown, Claro Extender *(USArtQuest/Jacquard)*
- cream colored brads
- rubber brayer
- felt applicator *(see page 12)*
- ⅛" (.3cm) hole punch
- Tulipa stamp *(Stamp Out Cute)*

Finished Size:
9¼" × 4½" **(23.5cm × 11.4cm)**

1 Ink the Stamp

Coat the stamp with a layer of black permanent ink and repeat with another layer. Immediately place the Tulipa stamp image side up and lay the acetate on top. Roll a clean brayer one way over the acetate to transfer the image. Pull off the acetate immediately.

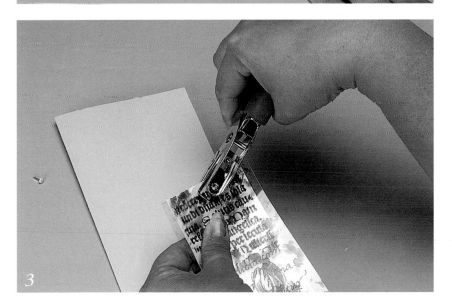

2 Add Spot Color to Punctuate

Apply adjacent drops of Burro, Havana Brown, and Claro Extender to the felt applicator. Spot color by pouncing onto the uninked side of the acetate. Add more ink as necessary.

3 Layer with Decorative Brads

Cut cream cardstock slightly narrower but the same length as the acetate piece. Punch holes at the center top and bottom and attach the two pieces together with cream brads. Layer onto folded peach cardstock with double-sided tape.

 **TRADE SECRET** *For a different look try adding Glaze Vernis on top of the acetate and then remove some of the ink with a dry textured stamp.* ■

VARIEGATION

Cut n' Dry Foam or Felt by Ranger is a great way to make a custom pad or a larger stamping surface. They both work well for paint and ink application. I quickly developed a preference for the foam sheets because their texture transferred to the bold stamps being used for the resist. The ability to mix different resist, dye and metallic inks together gave new life to my bolder stamps and has become one of my favorite techniques.

■ ■ ■ ■ MATERIALS LIST

- glossy white and purple cardstock
- bottled clear resist ink
- dye ink pads: Adirondacks in Caramel, Pesto, Eggplant *(Ranger)*
- metallic ink pad: Brilliance in Gold *(Tsukineko)*
- bottled dye re-inkers: Adirondacks in Caramel, Pesto, Butterscotch, Eggplant *(Ranger)*
- gold leafing pen
- gold brads
- Japanese hole punch or awl
- Cut n' Dry foam pad *(Ranger)*
- swoosh stamp *(Art Impressions)*
- ash leaf stamp *(Fred Mullett)*

Finished Size:
8½" × 4¼" **(21.6cm × 10.8cm)**

1 Add Resist Ink to Foam Pad

Add bottled clear resist ink to a piece of Cut n' Dry foam in a wave-like pattern.Choose a pleasing pattern and stick to it. It will then become easier to add the other combinations of dye ink around it.

2 Continue Inking the Pad With Dye Ink

Add drops of Pesto, Eggplant and Butterscotch re-inker colors to the pad, avoiding the area covered by the resist ink.

3 Stamp Textural Image

Using the stamp pad you just made, stamp a solid swoosh image on glossy cardstock. Repeat randomly throughout card.

4 Heat to Dry

Dry for fifteen to twenty seconds with a continuously moving heat tool. Flip the card over and blot it on a clean sheet of scrap paper to remove excess ink that did not dry.

5 Stain the Background

Apply Caramel and a bit of Pesto ink to a cosmetic sponge (either by pad or bottle). Rub in a linear motion from top to bottom to stain the rest of the background. Some of the ink may still be active from the stamping, but it will blend nicely with the other colors.

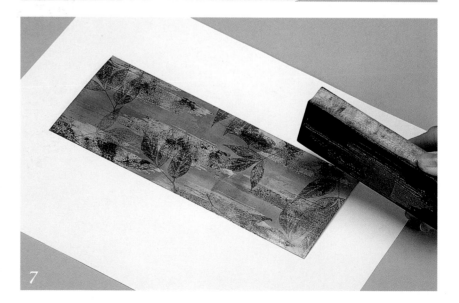

6 Stamp Top Layer

Stamp ash leaves randomly over the card in Pesto and Eggplant.

7 Stamp Metallic Highlights

Using a Gold Brilliance pad, stamp some more with the swoosh stamp to create highlights.

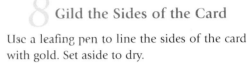 **Gild the Sides of the Card**

Use a leafing pen to line the sides of the card with gold. Set aside to dry.

9 Punch Holes Down Center

Measuring with a centering ruler, use a Japanese hole punch, set to an ⅛" (.3cm) diameter, and make three holes down the center of the stamped piece. Add gold brads and close. These will not attach to the folded cardstock, but serve as a decorative embellishment.

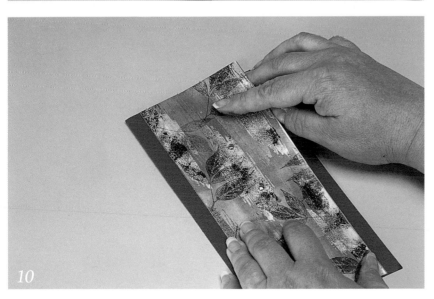

10 Mount to Finish

Mount the finished front onto purple cardstock with double-sided tape.

PEAR TILE

I spent some time exploring tissue paper overlays during my domino heyday. I was amazed that the overlays were virtually invisible on the dominoes and I loved the visual depth I got because the color was coming from behind. The concept works equally well to transform inexpensive white bathroom tile into decorative accents, coasters, magnets or art pieces.

■ ■ ■ ■ ■ MATERIALS LIST

- white ceramic tile
- tissue paper
- deli or waxed paper
- permanent ink pads: StazOn in Timber Brown, Olive Green *(Tsukineko)*
- gold leafing pen

- alcohol inks: Piñata in Burro Brown, Rainforest Green, Claro Extender *(USArtQuest/Jacquard)*
- matte finish spray
- floor finish in spray bottle
- clear satin polyurethane
- pecan satin varnish

- felt applicator *(see page 12)*
- pudgy pear stamp *(A Stamp in the Hand)*
- script background stamp *(A Stamp in the Hand)*

Finished Size:
4¼" × 4¼" **(10.8cm × 10.8cm)**

1 Prep and Spot Color Tile

Wipe the surface of the tile to clean. Spray with matte finish spray to prep. This gives a surface for the inks to stick to, and cuts down on chipping that may occur before the final sealing. Apply one to two adjacent drops of Rainforest Green and Burro Brown inks to a felt applicator. Quickly add one to two drops of Claro Extender to the same area on the felt and pounce on the tile to spot color.

2 Prepare Tissue Overlay

Cut a piece of plain white tissue to fit the top of the tile. Stamp onto the tissue with the script in Timber Brown and the pear in Olive Green. Let the ink dry for a couple of minutes before continuing. It is important that a non-smearing permanent ink be used for this project.

3 Adhere Tissue Overlay to Tile

Place the stamped tissue on top of the tile. Spray on floor finish and carefully smooth the tissue out with wetted fingers. Set aside to dry about twenty minutes.

4 Apply Protective Sealant

Use a cosmetic sponge to varnish with clear satin polyurethane. Set on waxed paper to dry. Spot on random bits of pecan varnish to shadow. This will dry in under an hour. If more color is desired, add a second coat.

5 Gild the Edges

Paint the edges of the tile with a gold leaf pen to give the piece a finished look.

 TRADE SECRET *Spray polyurethane is a good substitute for brush-on varnish, but generally requires more coats. It is also important to remember to protect your work surface before spraying.* ■

TILE MAGNETS

I love projects that are easily appropriate as gifts, or that are a starting point for series work. These magnets accomplish both. I usually work on these in stages, spot coloring many tiles at once and adding overlays later when needed. Go wild with your themes and soon you will be a magnet-making machine!

TECHNIQUE TACTIC *For projects where I am going to use a partial area of a stamp or background design I often make a template out of clear Mylar. I cut it to the size of my surface (in this case, a tile) and then move it around over the stamped image to pick exactly the right spot I want to use.* ■

■ ■ ■ ■ MATERIALS LIST

- 3 small white ceramic tiles
- adhesive-backed magnetic strips
- white tissue paper
- black permanent ink pad

- alcohol inks: Studio II Ink*Its in Canary Yellow *(Graphic Marker)*, Piñata in Rainforest Green, Purple Passion and Claro Extender *(USArtQuest/Jacquard)*
- gold leafing pen
- matte finish spray
- floor finish

- deli or waxed paper
- clear satin polyurethane
- pecan satin varnish
- felt applicator *(see page 12)*
- large travel stamp *(JudiKins)*

Finished Size:
1⅞" × 1⅞" (4.8cm × 4.8cm)

1 Prep and Spot Color Tiles

Prep tiles as directed on page 65 and apply one to two drops of Rainforest Green, Purple Passion, Canary Yellow, and Claro Extender inks to felt applicator. Pounce on all three tiles, leaving a few large areas of white space.

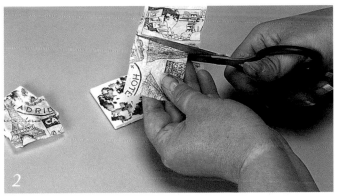

2 Stamp and Cut Images

Stamp large travel stamp on tissue paper using black permanent ink. Let dry for one to two minutes and then cut to fit the tops of the tiles.

3 Adhere Tissue Overlays to Tiles

Lay the cut images on the tiles and spray with floor finish. Smooth bubbles and wrinkles out with a wet finger.

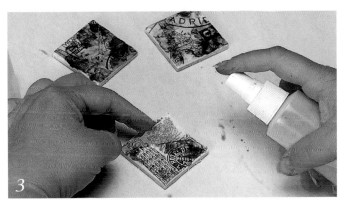

4 Seal the Tiles

Use a cosmetic sponge to pat on clear satin polyurethane or use several coats of spray varnish. Add pecan satin varnish to add color and create depth.

5 Gild Edges and Attach Magnets

Gild the edges with a leafing pen and cut and attach adhesive-backed magnets to the back of each tile. The business card size sheets of magnets are perfect for this project.

FLIGHTS OF FANCY

Sometimes play that mixes new techniques with old can lead to something really special. This was the case when I began mixing interference powdered pigments with alcohol inks. I had a lot of inspiration from other artists using those inks on white glossy cardstock, but wanted to put my own spin on it. I decided to try the combination on black glossy cardstock and was really pleased with the results.

■ ■ ■ ■ MATERIALS LIST

- black glossy and pale green cardstock
- black permanent ink pad
- metallic ink pads: Brilliance in Moonlight White *(Tsukineko)*
- alcohol inks: Studio II in Chartreuse, Yellow Green, Blender *(Graphic Marker)*

- powdered pigments: Interference Green, Interference Gold *(Pearl-Ex)*
- gold leafing pen
- gold gel pen
- gold metallic thread
- acrylic dragonfly
- 20-gauge gold wire

- E6000 adhesive
- round-nose pliers
- ¹⁄₁₆" (.2cm) hole punch
- felt applicator *(see page 12)*
- small dragonfly stamp *(Paper Inspirations)*

Finished Size:
4¼" × 9½" **(10.8cm × 24.1cm)**

1 Rub on Powdered Pigments

Rub spots of Interference Gold and Interference Green powdered pigments on black glossy cardstock.

2 Liquefy Pigments With Alcohol Inks

Using the homemade applicator, apply two to three adjacent drops of Chartreuse, Yellow Green and blender ink. Pounce the card following the path of the powdered pigments until they begin to liquefy and spread. Add more inks until all the powdered pigments have blended with the alcohol inks to make a variegated background. No sealing is necessary since the alcohol will act as the binder.

3 Stamp Dragonfly Background

After is it dry, stamp the background throughout with a small dragonfly stamp and black permanent ink.

4 Cut Stamped Background

Cut the background into five wavy-bordered sections. Place the pieces aside in their original order.

 TRADE SECRET *Interference pigments are mica-based colors with properties that interfere with how light is reflected and refracted. They appear only slightly tinted on white papers, but are really dramatic on dark papers, particularly black. I love to use them as an undercoat because they cause such a change in the appearance of the overpainted areas. Your choice of binders is huge and your imagination is your only limit on what you can do with them.* ■

5 Mount Sections

Mount the sections onto another, longer strip of glossy black cardstock using double-sided tape. Leave small gaps between each section to let the black show through.

6 Coat Acrylic Dragonfly

Coat the back of the acrylic dragonfly with Moonlight White. Dry with a heat tool. The white will provide contrast for the spot coloration in the next step.

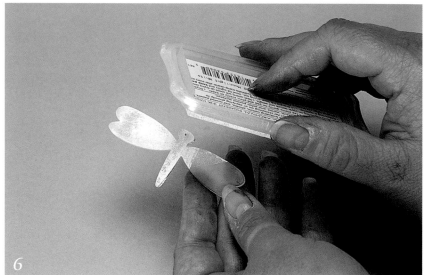

7 Spot Color the Dragonfly

Apply two drops of Chartreuse, Yellow Green and blender ink on the felt applicator. Using the gold leafing pen, add one dot on top of the inks and pounce the applicator on the front of the acrylic dragonfly to spot color. By varying the amount of blender ink, this becomes a spot coloration application of a background technique known as "polished stone."

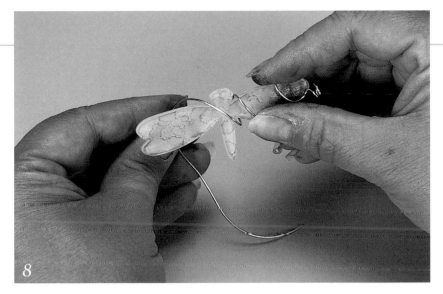

8 Add Wire to Embellishment

Wrap the dragonfly loosely with 20-gauge gold wire. Coil the ends with round-nosed pliers.

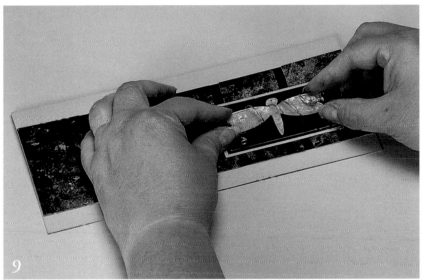

9 Adhere the Dragonfly

Mount the black glossy cardstock onto a folded piece of pale green cardstock. Cut a rectangular piece of black glossy cardstock slightly larger than the dragonfly. Cut a second piece to layer behind it. Spot color this second piece using the same process used on the dragonfly and attach with double-sided tape. Adhere the dragonfly with E6000.

10 Create a Tag and Attach

Cut a small tag out of scrap black glossy cardstock. Punch a 1/16" (.2cm) hole at the end and write the phrase with a gold gel pen. Tie onto gold wire with metallic thread and add double-sided tape to secure.

JOYFUL NOISE

The articles I read on this shaving cream marbling technique piqued my interest because the materials are readily available and the cleanup is quick. I also learned quickly that playing in the cream, to mingle the inks, is addictive. I now work with several piles of cream at a time because I am less tempted to overmix. In this case, less is more, and self-control is important.

■ ■ ■ ■ MATERIALS LIST

- cream linen and terra cotta cardstock
- dye ink re-inkers: Adirondacks in Ginger, Caramel, Red Pepper, Espresso (Ranger)
- antiqued brads

- art masking tape
- regular shaving cream
- rubber squeegee
- ⅛" (.3cm) hole punch
- stipple brush

- phrase stamp (Printworks)

Finished Size:
5¾" × 5½" (14.6cm × 14cm)

1 Mask for Marbling

Mask a piece of cream linen cardstock with torn art masking tape to form a small, loose square. Burnish the tape firmly around the inside of the square, to assure a good bond.

2 Prepare Shaving Cream

Spray a mound of regular shaving cream into a paper plate and smooth it out lightly with a squeegee or knife.

3 Drip Inks Onto Surface

Add two or three drops of Ginger, Red Pepper, and Caramel onto the shaving cream.

4 Swirl the Inks

Swirl the inks together into a marbled pattern with the end of a paintbrush or cocktail straw. The amount of mixing will determine the design, so play a little to determine your personal preference. Less mixing will result in little design, while over-mixing will muddy the marbling.

5 Dip Masked Paper Into Ink Mixture

Lightly press the masked part of the card into the marbling mixture and lift off.

6 Remove Shaving Cream to Reveal Pattern

Pull the rubber squeegee through the shaving cream in one motion to remove the shaving cream. Wipe off excess onto scrap paper and continue until all residue is gone.

7 Remove the Mask

With clean fingers, carefully peel off all sides of the mask.

 TECHNIQUE TACTIC An old credit card, plastic hotel key, or plastic scraper, are all good substitutes for the squeegee. The more flexible your tool is, the easier the removal will be. ■

8 Stipple for Added Texture

Use a stipple brush to lightly stipple the same inks to extend colors onto the cardstock outside of the masked area.

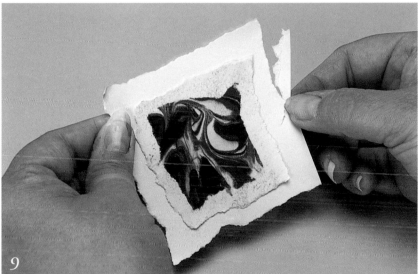

9 Tear Borders and Layer

Tear a border around the image and adhere the image to a larger piece of the same cream linen cardstock. Tear that piece as well to create an even larger torn border and repeat with a third piece. Adhere all three layers onto terra cotta cardstock with double-sided tape.

10 Stamp and Mount Sentiment

Use Espresso ink to stamp "Make a Joyful Noise" onto a small, torn piece of terra cotta cardstock. Use an ⅛" (.3cm) hole punch to punch brad holes at either end. Place antiqued brads then attach the phrase angled below the image with double-sided tape.

SCATTER JOY

Bigger projects are no more difficult to marble than small ones; they just need a larger workspace and a larger surface area of shaving cream. I spread enough cream so that the background only needs to be dipped once, maintaining the integrity of the initial pattern. I decided to soften the contrast by reapplying the scraped cream to tint the rest of the background here. That helped the marbling appear more water-like to fit the theme of the card.

■ ■ ■ ■ MATERIALS LIST

- white and dark blue cardstock
- adhesive-backed laminate sheet
- permanent ink pads: StazOn in Azure, Black *(Tsukineko)*
- metallic ink pads: Brilliance in Ice Blue, Platinum Planet *(Tsukineko)*

- dye inks: Nick Bantock in Cerulean Azure, Chartreuse Green, Prussian Blue *(Ranger)*
- decorative silver brads
- regular shaving cream
- ⅛" (.3cm) hole punch

- rubber squeegee
- shell stamp *(Rubber Poet)*
- phrase stamp *(Hero Arts)*

Finished Size:
4¼" × 9" **(10.8cm × 22.9cm)**

1 Add Inks to Shaving Cream Base

Spread and smooth a long strip of shaving cream onto your working surface. Drip four to five drops each, of Cerulean Azure, Chartreuse Green and Prussian Blue inks over the top surface of the cream.

2 Swirl the Inks

Swirl the inks together in a marbled pattern with the end of a paintbrush or with a small straw.

3 Press to Transfer Marbled Design

Lay the white cardstock on top of the shaving cream mixture and press down a little to be sure the entire card surface makes contact with it. Lift the paper off of the shaving cream.

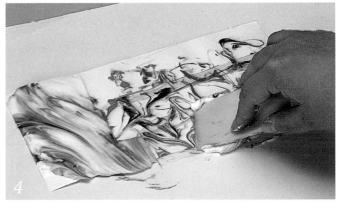

4 Remove Shaving Cream to Reveal Pattern

Use a squeegee to remove the excess shaving cream mixture from corner to corner. Wipe off excess and continue one-stroke removal until the paper is free of shaving cream. Blot any excess with a paper towel.

5 Stain Again with Shaving Cream Mix

To add some light color to the marbling, rub the used colored shaving cream mixture onto the paper and remove it again with the squeegee. The result will be a softer shade that complements the marbling.

6 Laminate the Background

Laminate the background sheet with clear adhesive-backed laminate. Use a bone folder to ensure a good bond throughout.

7 Stamp Pattern on Top

Stamp shell randomly over the laminate with Platinum Planet and Ice Blue Brilliance. Then stamp with the darker Azure and Black to bring out the shell detail. Finish by stamping the phrase in Black. Heat the inks to dry, keeping the heat tool about 12" (30.48cm) away from the laminate, or let dry for twenty-four hours.

8 Add Brads and Mount Layers

Using an ⅛" (.3cm) hole punch, punch three holes randomly below the phrase and attach three decorative silver brads. Attach the laminate piece to a slightly larger piece of white cardstock with double-sided tape. Then layer onto dark blue cardstock to finish.

VARIATION:
FRAGMENTS

The centerpiece of this card is a laminate transfer of a stamped playing card. Paint, stamp, tear and label a playing card, then take it to make a color copy of it. Burnish the copy to the laminate, soak and roll off the excess paper, leaving the toner. Layer the piece onto a frame of cardstock and attach to the background cardstock along with two pieces of coiled wire.

VARIATION:
RETRO

To make a retro/sixties look for this journal cover, stamp the retro images in resist ink and dry. Place tissue shapes in the open areas and activate the tissue with a bit of water. Dry the paper and add more stamping in fun dye ink colors. Apply a copper leafing pen directly to the stamps and stamp for a final layer. This is also an effective way to spot color. Attach the finished glossy piece to book board and coil-bind it to finish.

SURFACE
ALTERATION

Visual texture lets our eyes "feel" the surfaces created by an artist's imagination. This chapter explores this design element by using white space, overpatterning, high contrast and distressing. Each technique is capable of creating its own mood and can be widely used in paper arts and mixed media projects.

I love distressed looks because they remind me of times long past. Partial inkings are an easy technique that bring a vintage mood to the artwork. Walnut and white inks are two of my tried-and-true ways to create a classic look, but a recent discovery of the wonders of masking tape has allowed me to create some very interesting palette stamped pieces.

High-contrast designs with repeated motifs are intense and exciting. Many different color combinations and shapes can achieve this effect. Complementary colors provide intense contrast, while analogous colors result in a look that is much softer.

Overpatterning in metallic ink is another way I like to create subtle texture. I add this over the first layer of artwork to unify and finish a design. I've found a mesh brayer to be handy, but there are many larger background stamps that will produce the same effect.

BOTANICA PALETTE

I have been a big fan of chalk inks since their arrival on the scene. A distressed look complements their properties, but I found that taking the pad directly to the paper didn't give the look I wanted. Masking tape has become my way to add the inks where and how I want them. It adds a texture all its own while leaving the desired white space to create that distressed look.

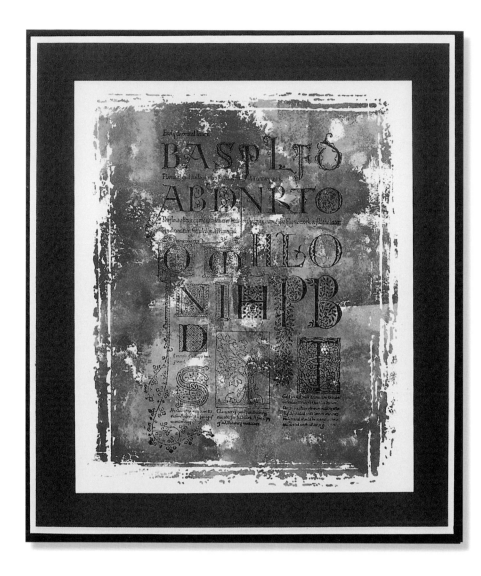

■ ■ ■ **MATERIALS LIST**

- white, black, green cardstock
- black permanent ink pad

- chalk ink pads: ColorBox Fluid Chalk pads in Deep Green, Olive Pastel *(Clearsnap)*
- masking tape

- fancy alphabet stamp *(Treasure Cay)*
- palette stamp *(Stampers Anonymous)*

Finished Size:
6¼" × 5½" **(15.9cm × 14cm)**

1 Add Color Spots to Stamp

Tap small areas of a palette stamp with the Deep Green chalk pad. Leave some of the areas uninked to accept other colors.

2 Press Tape Into Ink Pad

Press the sticky side of a 4" to 5" (10.2cm to 12.7cm) strip of masking tape into an Olive Pastel chalk pad.

3 Spot Color With Tape

Press the inked side of the tape onto the palette stamp. Move and repeat. If more ink is needed or a third color is desired, use a fresh piece of tape to avoid contaminating the chalk pad. The goal is to leave some uninked areas that will eventually have a soft, distressed look once stamped.

TEXTURE TIDBIT *Textural effects from rubber stamps can be a dramatic addition to the background if a third color is introduced, or they can be mingled with the other inks in a neutral or similar color for a subtler approach. Bolder textured stamps will make more of a statement because more surface area will be added to the palette. Finer-lined stamps will be more of a background accent and will be less noticeable to the eye unless a dramatic color is chosen.* ■

4 Stamp Inked Palette

Stamp the palette stamp onto matte-finish cardstock. Use a heat tool to dry and set.

5 Add Text Stamp

Use black permanent ink to stamp the alphabet stamp onto the chalk background.

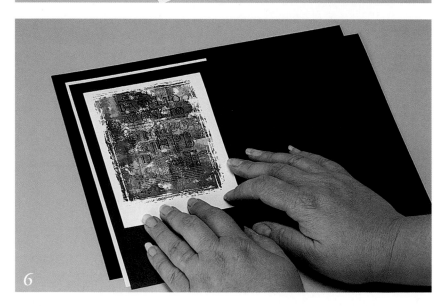

6 Mount Layers

Select and mount layers to create a framed border for the card. I chose colors that matched the inks in this card, but layering with complements or other accent colors can enhance the stamped center image.

VARIATION:

TUSCAN COLUMN

■ ■ ■ ■

MATERIALS LIST

- light brown, light purple, black cardstock
- black permanent ink pad
- chalk ink pads: ColorBox Fluid Chalk pads in Yellow Ochre, Wisteria *(Clearsnap)*
- masking tape
- large palette stamp *(Stampers Anonymous)*
- architectural stamp *(A Stamp in the Hand)*
- splotches stamp *(Art Impressions)*

Finished Size:
6¾" × 5½" **(17cm × 14cm)**

1 Spot Color Palette Stamp

Tear a 4" to 5" (10.2cm to 12.7 cm) piece of masking tape and press into the Wisteria pad. Lightly press the tape onto the large palette stamp and remove. Repeat to spot color throughout. Tear a second piece of tape and add accents with Yellow Ochre in the same manner.

Ink a splotches stamp with Yellow Ochre and stamp directly onto the palette stamp. This will intensify the ochre in certain spots.

2 Stamp Inked Palette

Stamp a piece of matte cardstock with the inked palette stamp.

3 Stamp Focal Image

Stamp the architectural image with permanent black ink. Use double-sided tape to attach the stamped piece to light purple, black and light brown cardstock to finish.

VINTAGE SHOES

Adding texture over a design can add so much to a composition. Sometimes I use textural stamps to achieve this, but my favorite tool has become a mesh brayer. I've found that I prefer metallic ink so that the mesh is there to enhance, not distract. Bold images underneath provide the greatest contrast and tend to produce the best results.

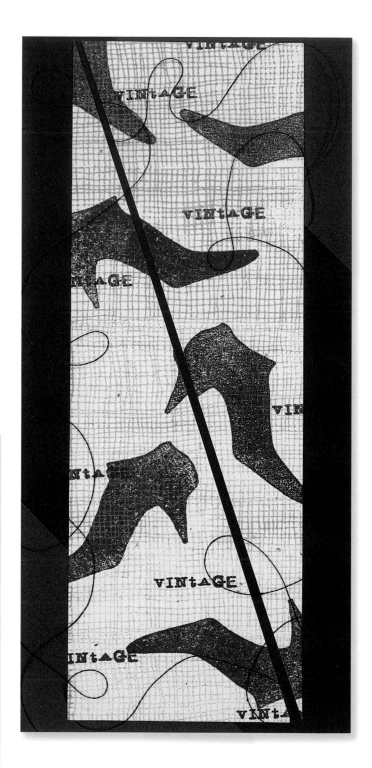

■ ■ ■ MATERIALS LIST

- white confetti, brown and red cardstock
- dye ink pads: Nick Bantock in Rose Madder, Van Dyke Brown, Vermillion Lacquer (Ranger)
- metallic ink pad: Encore Metallic Gold (Tsukineko)
- maroon metallic fiber
- paper adhesive, matte
- matte finish spray
- mesh brayer (Fiskars)
- shoe stamp (Alextamping)
- "Vintage" stamp (Treasure Cay)

Finished Size:
8¾" × 4¼" (22.2cm × 10.8cm)

1 Stamp Background Design

Stamp shoe randomly on speckled cardstock using Rose Madder, Van Dyke Brown and Vermillion Lacquer.

2 Brayer Over Design

Ink a mesh brayer with gold metallic ink. Brayer over the entire design, using one continuous motion. Heat to dry or seal with two light coats of matte sealer.

3 Add Word Stamp

Stamp the word "Vintage" around the shoes using the same colors. This could also be stamped before the metallic ink was added.

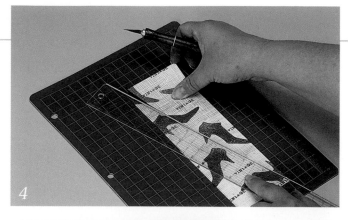

4 Make a Diagonal Cut

Cut the card diagonally from corner to corner using a cutting mat and a craft knife.

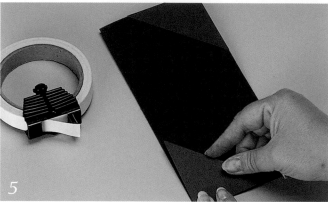

5 Cut Triangles for Mounting

Cut two equal-sized triangles out of brown cardstock, and mount using double-sided tape to the opposite corners of a long red card.

6 Mount and Adhere Metallic Fiber

Lift up one of the brown corners and stick the end of the maroon fiber to the tape. Press down to ensure a good bond. Place double-sided tape on the decorated card and lightly place the split image on the card front. Loop the fiber around the card surface, following the natural direction that the fiber tends to curl, and glue them down where they want to fall naturally. Adhere with dots of paper adhesive applied with a small brush.

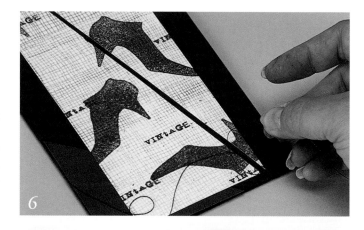

7 Tuck Fiber Ends to Finish

Tuck the ends under the top image and press the card front down to finish the card.

VARIATION:
SUMMER FLORAL

■ ■ ■ ■

MATERIALS LIST

- cream linen, goldenrod cardstock
- chalk ink pads. ColorBox Fluid Chalk pads in Bisque, Dark Moss *(Clearsnap)*
- metallic ink pads: Champagne Encore Metallic *(Tsukineko)*
- mesh brayer *(Fiskars)*
- shadow stamp row *(Hero Arts)*
- daisy stamp *(Impression Obsession)*

Finished Size:
4½" × 8½" **(11.4cm × 21.6cm)**

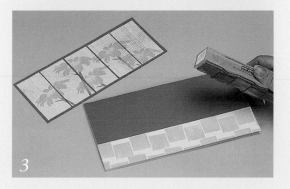

1 Stamp Daisy Images

Ink daisy with Dark Moss and Bisque and stamp randomly on the cream linen cardstock. Add mesh texture with brayer using Champagne metallic ink. Use a heat tool to set.

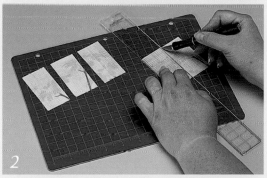

2 Cut Into Five Panels

Measure using a ruler and cut the background into five equal panels. Mount onto a slightly larger piece of goldenrod cardstock.

3 Stamp a Border and Mount

With the shadow row stamp and Bisque, create a coordinating border on a narrow strip of cream linen cardstock. Heat to set with a heat tool. Adhere to the bottom of the folded card front with double-sided tape. Then adhere the five-paneled piece to a larger goldenrod piece and layer that onto the folded card to finish.

ETERNAL STYLE

Chalk inks can produce a soft look when used with detail stamps. Sometimes I like to soften that look even further by adding another layer of images stamped with white or off-white ink. Add a lot for a vintage look, or less for a more ethereal quality. There is such a wide variety of looks that can be acheived.

■■■ MATERIALS LIST

- cream linen, medium brown and sage green cardstock
- chalk ink pads: ColorBox Fluid Chalk pads in Dark Moss, Yellow Ochre, Chestnut Roan, Alabaster *(Clearsnap)*

- ash stamp *(Fred Mullett)*
- fern stamp *(OM Studio)*
- branch stamp *(Love to Stamp)*

- phrase stamp *(Hero Arts)*

Finished Size:
5½" × 5½" (14cm × 14cm)

1 Drag Pad to Spot Color

Drag a Dark Moss pad over a piece of cream linen cardstock. Leave some areas uninked.

2 Stamp Leaves to Create Background

Stamp ash leaves in Yellow Ochre and Chestnut Roan. Stamp fern in Dark Moss and Chestnut Roan. Stamp branch in Yellow Ochre. Heat to set with a heat tool.

3 Distress Background

Stamp over with all of the images using Alabaster. This will further distress the background in a subtle way. A stark white pad would create a more obvious distressed look.

4 Cut Into Panels

Cut the image into five equal panels and layer them on top of the medium brown cardstock with double-sided tape.

5 Add Phrase to the Card Front

Stamp the edges of a folded sage green cardstock with the style phrase in Chestnut Roan. Heat to set and then attach layered panels with double-sided tape to finish.

TRADE SECRET Keep chalk ink pads well inked for easier application. These pads tend to act "drier" than other pigment pads. ■

DREAM BOX

Decorating a box should be quick and easy, and it can be with the right materials and techniques. Splattering and sponging are a great way to cover surface area quickly, yet create a rough look that is a perfect background for the next layer of stamping. Since a box's surface makes stamping challenging, I choose stamps that will look naturally distressed if accidental partial stampings occur. Mix this with metallic accents and you'll have an eye-catching box for display.

▪ ▪ ▪ MATERIALS LIST

- white papier-mâché box
- five wooden ¾" (1.9cm) blocks
- permanent ink pads: StazOn in Timber Brown, Royal Purple *(Tsukineko)*
- dye ink pads: Adirondacks in Eggplant, Currant, Pesto, Espresso
- metallic ink pads: Brilliance in Copper *(Tsukineko)*

- walnut drawing ink
- copper leafing pen
- gold dream tag
- small luggage tag
- colorful fibers
- E6000 adhesive
- paper adhesive
- toothbrush

- color duster
- spray bottle with water
- oak print stamp *(Impression Obsession)*
- poetic oak leaves print stamp *(Hero Arts)*
- alphabet stamp *(Moon Rose)*

Finished Size: 4½" × 4½" × 3½" **(11.4cm × 11.4cm × 8.26cm)**

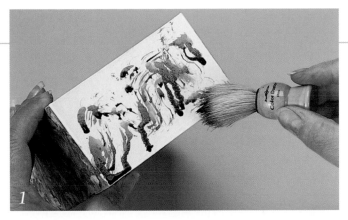

1 Stain Box With Walnut Ink

Use a color duster to dab walnut drawing ink over the surface of the papier-mâché box.

2 Move the Ink

Use a cosmetic sponge to move the ink around. Leave some white space and let air dry.

3 Splatter Box With Dye Inks

Ink any small stamp with Eggplant ink and stamp into the inkpad lid. Spritz lid once with water to dilute. Dip in a toothbrush and spatter the box, concentrating on the lower half.

4 Deepen the Color With More Ink

Spatter a second layer using diluted Currant ink and the same toothbrush. Bring the unwashed toothbrush closer this time to concentrate the spatters in small areas. Spatter a final coat with diluted Pesto ink using a clean toothbrush. Let dry thoroughly or dry with a heat tool.

TECHNIQUE TACTIC *The dye from re-inker bottles can be diluted for spattering much in the same way as the ink from a pad. Place a drop or two in a cup or on a piece of waxed or deli paper and spritz with water.* ■

5 Stamp Design on Box

Stamp the box sides with Timber Brown ink using the poetic oak leaves stamp. Add metallic highlights with the smaller oak print stamp in Copper ink. Heat to dry.

6 Stamp Alphabet Parts

To create a broken text effect, ink only parts of the alphabet stamp with Royal Purple. Concentrate the stamping in the lighter areas of the box.

7 Stain Box Lid With Dye

Stain the lid by sponging on a mix of Pesto and Eggplant inks with a cosmetic sponge.

8 Add Metallic to Box Lid

Use the Copper pad to cover the lid of the box with metallic ink. Heat to dry.

9 Stamp Box Lid Design

Stamp leaves on the box lid with Espresso. (The stamping will appear dark at first, but it will fade upon drying to create a subtle, background design.)

10 Stamp Small Luggage Tag

Using the same dye inks, stamp the small luggage tag with both leaf stamps and the alphabet stamp. Stamp the poetic leaf once in Copper and heat to dry. Attach a mixture of fibers and the gold metal "dream" embellishment to the tag. Use paper adhesive and a paintbrush to tack down fibers where desired.

11 Add Cubes to Finish

Use copper leafing pen to color cubes. Attach four to the box bottom for feet and one to the center of the top lid with E6000.

CHASING DIAMONDS

Harlequin design is a motif I return to frequently because of its classic look. I also like the elegance of black-and-white art, so a combination of the two is a natural fit. The webbing, black ink and white paint work well to create contrast, while repeating some of the designs adds unity. This design is very effective in other color combinations. Pick some favorites and give them a try.

■ ■ ■ MATERIALS LIST

- black and white cardstock
- black permanent ink pad
- acrylic paint: Glaze Vernis in Linen White *(Plaid)*
- black webbing spray

- swirl stamp *(Great Impressions)*
- tag stamp *(Hero Arts)*
- solid diamond stamp *(Rubber Tree)*

- checkerboard stamp *(Moon Rose)*

Finished Size:
7⅞" × 5½" **(20cm × 14cm)**

1 Ink a Solid Diamond Stamp

Ink a solid diamond stamp with black permanent ink. Tap off on scrap paper. Repeat inking

2 Apply Paint to Second Stamp

Using a cosmetic sponge, apply a thin coating of Linen White glaze to the checkerboard stamp. The use of the glaze will add more texture and contrast than using a white ink.

3 Stamp the Pattern Onto the Diamond

Lightly press the checkerboard stamp onto the freshly inked diamond stamp.

4 Stamp the Diamond

Press firmly to stamp the diamond onto white cardstock.

5 Stamp More Diamonds

Stamp more diamonds using different textured stamps. Stamp three plain black diamonds for contrast.

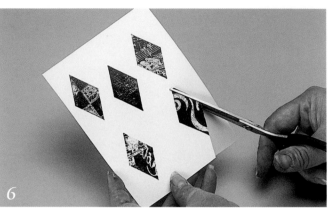

6 Cut Diamonds Out and Spray Webbing

Cut the diamonds out with scissors. Spray black webbing over the solid black diamonds and over the surface of a larger sheet of white cardstock.

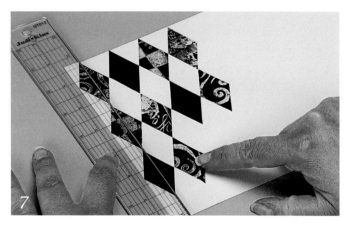

7 Mount the Diamonds

Use a ruler and double-sided tape to align and mount the diamonds onto white cardstock. Intermix the solid black diamonds among the patterned diamonds in a harlequin pattern of three down and four across.

8 Assemble the Card

Layer the diamond piece onto a slightly larger piece of black cardstock. Mount that onto the webbed, folded piece of white cardstock with double-sided tape.

 TECHNIQUE TACTIC *Another way to create diamonds is to create a large textured background, and use a decorative diamond punch to make the shapes.*

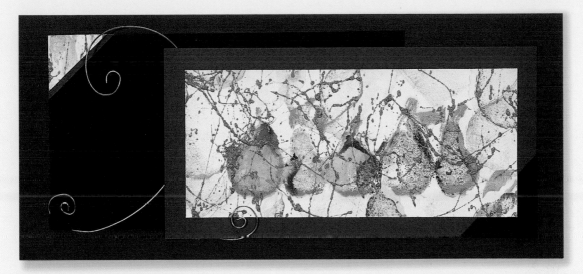

VARIATION:

FAMILY OF PEARS

To make this pretty pear card, randomly stamp partial images of single pears on a piece of white cardstock. Stamp a pear grouping in the center and then overstamp and emboss with gold embossing powder. To add more texture to the design, spray gold webbing before layering the card onto a slightly larger piece of green cardstock. Mount a piece of black cardstock behind the green piece and add wire between the two pieces for an interesting effect. Add left-over triangles of the decorated and the green cardstock in the upper left corner of the black cardstock to finish.

VARIATION:

PEARS ON PARADE

This card mixes inks and paints for variety. Ink the bold pear stamp with StazOn Olive, and then impress the design with Yellow Ochre acrylic paint before stamping onto the tinted tags. Add personality to the different images and create dimension by adding the tag letter stickers and round, antiqued brads. Layor on the black paper to make the center pop and to create an unusual mounting to make the card unique.

WATER
PLAY

My mother used to give me house painting brushes and a bucket of water to occupy my time when I was little. I can't tell you how many times my driveway was painted, but apparently a fascination with water and imagined paint began for me then. I love the fluidity of watercolor along with its transparency. The same properties that engage me can also be frustrating, but I plan projects that have great margins for error.

Single color or graduated washes are a great way to begin to play with these paints, while printing techniques will produce a variegated background and are easy to do. I've played around with a lot of different paper options and have found that coated papers will allow for some surface alteration before layering with more concentrated paints and inks. It is really exciting to watch the pattern build with each new layer. My favorite technique is pointilism, because of the endless color choices and variegated nature. It is great as a base design for many projects, or a wonderful doodling tool in art journals. It also takes me back to my roots: a brush with water and surface area to be covered. I am glad to have found my childhood whimsy again.

LOVE IS BLUE

When the batik resist technique burst onto the scene, I knew I had to try it. The movement of the watercolor goes very well with the natural flow of the paper fibers. I like to initially play with colors on scrap mulberry paper to see what combinations will work well with the batik designs. Experiment with different combinations to get the look you want.

■ ■ ■ ■ ■ MATERIALS LIST

- white, lavender and blue cardstock
- white mulberry paper
- waxy palette paper
- embossing pad
- dye ink pad: Adirondack in Denim *(Ranger)*
- metallic ink pad: Brilliance in Platinum *(Tsukineko)*

- watercolor paint: Dr. Ph. Martin's Hydrus in Phthalo Blue, Ultramarine, Payne's Gray, Cobalt Violet *(Salis International)*
- clear embossing powder
- 3" (7.5cm) foam brush
- paper adhesive
- silver brads
- coffee filter

- newsprint
- spray bottle, filled with water
- iron
- 1/8" (.3cm) hole punch
- spiral heart stamps *(Hero Art)*
- alphabet stamps *(Hero Art)*
- love stamp *(Eureka)*

Finished Size:
6" × 10" (15.2cm × 25.4cm)

1 Stamp Hearts Across Mulberry Paper

Stamp alternating hearts across the center of the mulberry paper in an overlapping pattern with the embossing ink.

2 Pour Embossing Powder

Pour embossing powder over the hearts and tap off excess into a coffee filter. Funnel powder back into jar.

3 Emboss

Heat to emboss the powder thoroughly with a heat tool. Be sure that all parts of the hearts have a shiny finish before finishing with the heat tool.

4 Spritz Mulberry Paper

Place the mulberry paper on waxy palette paper or a thick stack of newspaper. Wet the mulberry paper thoroughly with a spray bottle of water. This will accelerate the movement of the water-color throughout the mulberry paper.

5 Drop Watercolor Onto Brush

Dampen a 3" (7.5cm) foam brush and add two to three drops of Phthalo Blue Hydrus watercolor.

6 Paint Mulberry Paper

Brush onto dampened mulberry paper in a sweeping motion. Repeat until area is filled.

7 Blend in a Second Color

Clean the brush in water and add two to three drops of Ultramarine watercolor. Brush on to add secondary color to the mulberry paper.

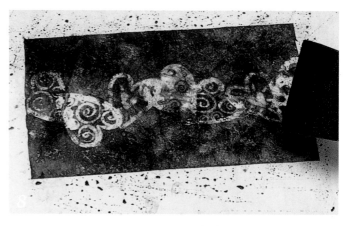

8 Spot Color to Shadow

Clean brush. Add a drop of Payne's Gray to one end of the brush and a drop of Cobalt Violet to the other end. Spritz to wet further. Add to background in small areas to shade. If needed, spritz the mulberry paper for more movement or to dilute area.

9 Wet Tear for a Feathered Edge

Gently tear an edge on the top and bottom while the paper is still damp. Set aside to dry.

 TRADE SECRET This type of watercolor project will produce more dramatic results if highly pigmented, artist quality paints are used. Watercolors with less pigment will require more layers to achieve the same vibrant color, but they will work with patience. Since this is a resist technique, darker colors and bolder designs will provide more contrast. Keep in mind that the watercolor will soften and lighten when it dries. ■

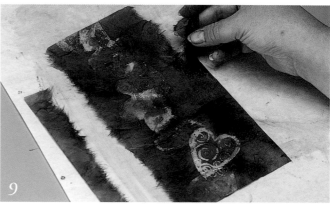

10 Use Heat to Remove Embossing Powder

Place mulberry paper between two sheets of newsprint and iron slowly to melt and remove embossing powder. Move the paper quickly while it is hot to avoid sticking and then place clean sheets of newsprint down again to repeat until all of the embossed areas are gone. Areas will look matte clear when all the powder has been removed.

11 Stamp and Cut Letters

Stamp lower case letters on scrap lavender paper in Denim ink. Cut each letter out and set aside.

12 Trim and Mount Dyed Mulberry

Use a hole punch to punch a hole on the left and right side of the batiked mulberry paper. Mount the mulberry to a piece of white cardstock with silver brads. Trim the sides as needed.

13 Stamp Folded Card

Stamp "love" using Platinum Brilliance around the perimeter of the folded blue card. Heat to set with a heat tool.

14 Mount Layers and Glue Letters to Finish

Continue building layers by mounting the batiked piece onto lavender cardstock and finally onto the folded blue card. Use paper adhesive to glue the cut letters at odd angles to finish.

ILLUMINATION

Combining watercolor with inks on coated surfaces can create a beautiful, muted design. I like to work in layers that add and subtract images, combining those with stamps that follow a theme. I use the background images pulled from the wash to support the added, more detailed, layers on top. A final ink layer creates focal interest where needed.

▪▪▪▪ MATERIALS LIST

- white and deep purple cardstock
- posterboard
- dye ink pad: Adirondack in Eggplant *(Ranger)*
- watercolor crayons: Aquacolor in Blue-Violet, Magenta *(Lyra)*
- 3" (7.5cm) foam brush

- spray bottle
- shadow stamp *(Hero Arts)*
- text stamp *(Limited Edition)*
- circus diamonds stamp *(Hampton Art Stamps)*
- moth chart stamp *(A Stamp in the Hand)*

- batik dragonfly stamp *(Paper Inspirations)*
- "Illumination" stamp *(Postmodern Design)*

Finished Size:
7½" × 5½" (19.1cm × 14cm)

1 Apply Watercolor Paint to Brush

Dampen a 3" (7.5cm) foam brush with water. Rub Blue-Violet and Magenta crayons on the edge of the brush until it is well coated. Spritz with a little more water to liquefy the crayon a bit further.

2 Apply Watercolor Wash

Run the wet brush horizontally over the coated side of a cut piece of posterboard. Repeat further down until totally covered. The posterboard will want to bend a little, but will calm down once dried.

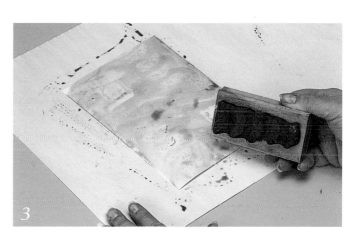

3 Create Design by Removing Paint

Quickly stamp into the paint with the dry moth, diamond, shadow and dragonfly stamps to create a reverse design. Tap off stamps each time to ensure the stamp is dry before continuing. I like to have all my stamps ready and my design in my head before wetting the paper with the wash. The process must be done quickly before the paint begins to sink into the coating.

4 Add to the Design With Stamps

Lightly mist the diamond stamp with water and color on the stamp with the Blue-Violet crayon. Stamp onto some of the open areas and repeat with the moth and dragonfly stamps.

5 Add the Final Ink Layer

Overstamp the moth, diamond, and text stamps in Eggplant ink.

6 Tear Undermount Paper

Dry tear a narrow strip of white cardstock. Mount it along the left side of the deep purple cardstock with double-sided tape.

7 Mount and Add Focal Stamp

Trim the posterboard design to size and center mount on the front of the card. Stamp "Illumination" on the right side of the design so that it rests outside of the white undermount and provides balance.

VARIATION:
THE KEY POINT

■ ■ ■ ■ ■

MATERIALS LIST

- brown and black cardstock
- white posterboard
- dye ink: Adirondack Espresso *(Ranger)*
- watercolor crayon: Aquacolor in Van Dyke Brown *(Lyra)*
- 3" (7.5cm) foam brush
- gate key stamp *(Limited Edition)*
- mosaic squares stamp *(Limited Edition)*
- dictionary stamp *(Moon Rose)*
- king stamp *(Stampers Anonymous)*
- text stamp *(Hero Arts)*
- checkerboard stamp *(Moon Rose)*
- "art" stamp *(Moon Rose)*

Finished Size:
8½" × 4¼" **(21.6cm × 10.8cm)**

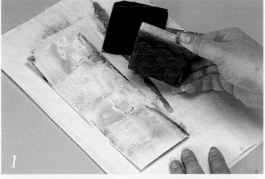

1 Apply Wash and Remove

Cut posterboard to size. Dampen a 3" (7.5cm) foam brush and load with Van Dyke Brown watercolor crayon. Apply wash and stamp dry checkerboard and mosaic squares stamps to remove design. Add back partial designs by wetting and adding Van Dyke Brown crayon to the mosaic, king, dictionary and text stamps.

2 Stamp With Darker Ink

Stamp gate key, "art" stamp, and dictionary stamp with Espresso Adirondack to finish the design. Mount on medium brown and black cardstock.

PIANO HINGE TAG BOOK

These little tag books have a winning combination: they're small and easy to do, with materials that are easy to find. I like to make them on glossy paper with watercolor, but they can be decorated with inks and paints, or just done in decorative paper. These covers were easily done as a print and then stamped with dye inks to coordinate. Wire, fibers and beads accent and add elegance to the spine for a unique presentation.

▪ ▪ ▪ ▪ MATERIALS LIST

- glossy cardstock
- 2" × 10" (5.1cm × 25.4cm) translucent vellum
- waxy palette paper
- dye ink pads: Adirondacks in Red Pepper, Terra Cotta, Espresso; Nick Bantock in Van Dyke Brown *(Ranger)*
- watercolors: Dr. Ph. Martin's Hydrus in Brilliant Cad Red, Hansa Deep Yellow, Gamboge *(Salis International)*

- seed beads
- thin rust fiber
- 24-gauge gold wire
- self-stick hole protectors
- tag pattern
- 3" (7.5cm) foam brush
- spray bottle, filled with water
- round-nosed pliers
- ¼" (.6cm) hole punch
- triangle stamp *(Fruit Basket Upset)*
- text stamp *(Limited Edition)*

- harlequin scrap stamp *(Stampers Anonymous)*
- mosaic stamp *(Stampers Anonymous)*
- alphabet stamps *(Handprint by Turtle Press)*
- time stamp *(Stampers Anonymous)*
- checkerboard stamp *(Stampers Anonymous)*
- splotch stamp *(Art Impressions)*

Finished Size:
2⅜" × 2" (6cm × 5.1cm)

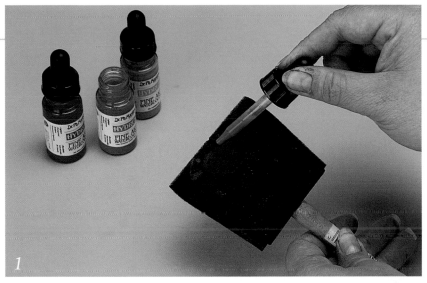

1 Load Brush With Paint

Dampen a 3" (7.5cm) foam brush and add two drops each of Brilliant Cad Red, Hansa Deep Yellow and Gamboge onto it.

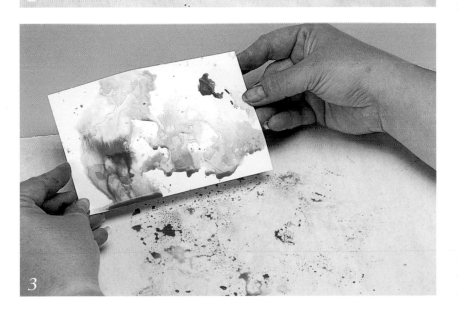

2 Apply Paint to Slick Surface

Tap the brush to apply paint to a slick surface. I used a waxy palette in this project, but have also achieved good results using glossy magazine paper. Experiment and decide which results you like best.

3 Dip Cardstock

Dip a piece of glossy cardstock, gloss side down, into the paint mixture. Lift up and allow to dry.

4 Cut Cover Using Template

Cut out the painted cardstock cover with scissors and a craft knife using the template provided on page 115. The painted side should be facing up. Tracing the pattern onto clear mylar and then using that as your template will enable you to see the painted surface and position as desired for cutting.

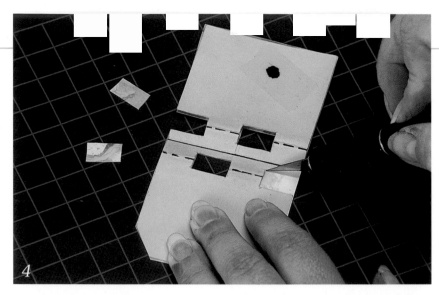

5 Stamp and Add Hole

Stamp the front and back cover with the harlequin scrap, triangle, text, checkerboard and clock face stamps using Red Pepper. Use the template again to punch a hole in the cover using a ¼" (.6m) punch.

6 Make Center Fold in Tag

Set tag horizontally with punch hole to the right. Fold toward the left and crease in the center with a bone folder. This will produce a "v" or valley fold.

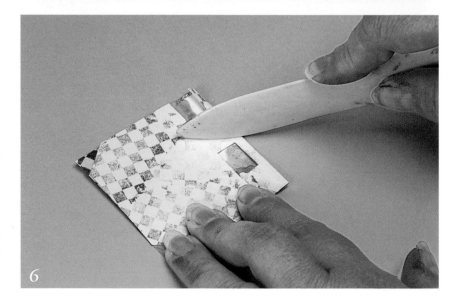

7 Fold at Midpoints of Hinge Holes

Open the tag cover. Folding right, crease at the midpoint of both sets of hinge holes. These will be "m" or mountain folds.

8 Fold Cover

This picture shows the folds as they should appear before putting the book together. When completely folded the hinges should fit together. The thickness of the paper or the hand cutting can change the alignment of the hinges. If that happens, just snip where needed so that they fit.

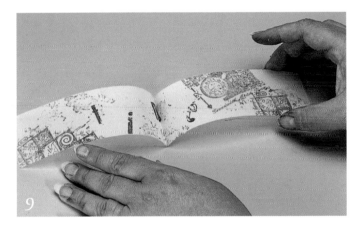

9 Decorate and Begin Folding Inside Pages

Create a background on the vellum strip by stamping alphabet letters, time, mosaic, and splotches with Van Dyke Brown, Red Pepper, Espresso, and Terra Cotta. Place design face up and fold in half (valley fold). Crease with a bone folder.

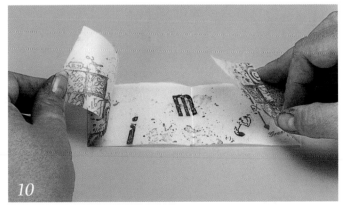

10 Fold Outsides Into Valley

Open first fold and fold the outside edges into the valley you created. Crease with a bone folder.

11 Turn Over and Fold Again

Turn the vellum over while still folded. Fold both sides into the center and crease again with a bone folder.

12 Fold Final Sections

Still folded from the last step, fold the last sections to the center. The result will be an accordion fold booklet with two central pages. If a third page is desired, fold the beginning valley fold with the design side down and continue with the same process.

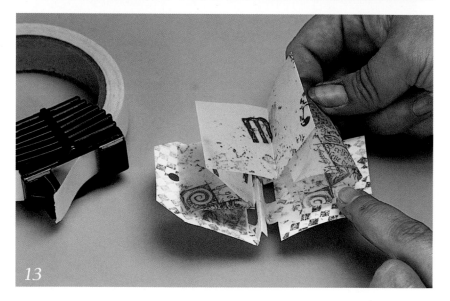

13 Attach Pages Inside Book

Use double-sided tape to attach the vellum pages inside the book. The ends of the paper should be near the spine.

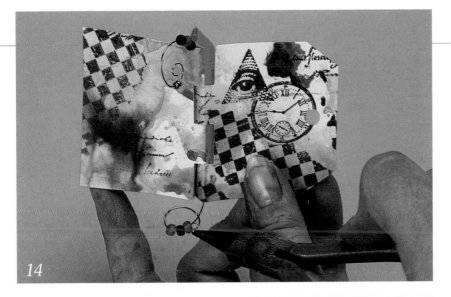

14 Add Wire to Hinge

Cut a 5" to 6" (12.7cm to 15.2cm) piece of 24-gauge wire and thread it through the hinges. Start at the top and add several beads before coiling with round-nose pliers in the natural direction of the wire. Add beads to the bottom and coil wire. Be sure to crimp the ends so that the beads will stay on.

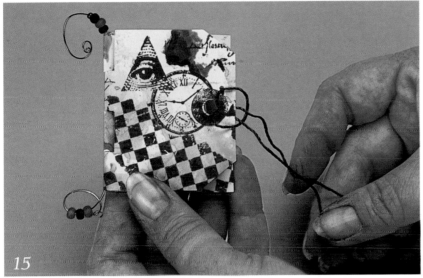

15 Add Protectors and Fiber

Color two self-stick hole protectors with Red Pepper and place on either side of the punched hole. Cut a 36" (9.18m) piece of thin, rust fiber and loosely knot through hole. Wrap around book and tuck to finish.

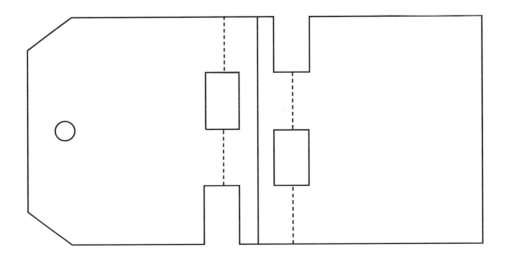

MONET'S SEASCAPE

I do a lot of art on the run these days and this pointillism technique came out of my mobile life. It is portable, mindless and somehow therapeutic if you enjoy just doodling with a brush, yet it looks like a lot of thought and fuss went into it. Best of all it is no-fail and doesn't require any special paper or planning. Scribble away and create your own masterpieces.

■ ■ ■ ■ ■ MATERIALS LIST

- glossy cardstock and white-speckled cardstock
- dye ink pad: Nick Bantock in Prussian Blue *(Ranger)*

- watercolor crayons: Aquacolor in Light Blue, Veridian, Moss Green, Peacock Blue; Blue-Violet, Apple Green *(Lyra)*
- gold leafing pen
- double-stick tape
- foam tape for layering

- Niji waterbrush *(Yasutomo)*
- deckle-edged scissors
- shell stamp *(Impression Obsession)*

  Finished Size:
  6" × 5½" **(15.2cm × 14cm)**

1 Apply Watercolor Crayon

Using the side of the Light Blue crayon, scribble in a thick zigzag pattern across the top of the glossy cardstock.

2 Liquefy Crayon

Use the Niji waterbrush in a pouncing motion to imitate pointillism and liquefy the crayon backgrounds. The first pounces will have larger amounts of water, but as the pigment collects on the brush, more pigment will build up adding more contrast. Blot if necessary until just damp. The watercolor will sit on top of the cardstock, yet stain it. Clean the brush out by lightly squeezing the barrel.

3 Add Two More Colors

Apply the Veridian and then the Moss Green crayons, using the same zigzag pattern just under the liquefied area.

4 Liquefy and Blend Colors

Liquefy the newly added colors and blot. Begin blending the colors together by pouncing on the darkly pigmented areas in one section and moving to the next area. This will produce a variegated background of lights and darks. If more contrast is needed, you can add more color by taking the color off the crayon with the waterbrush and adding it in directly.

5 Add Color Around All Sides

Continue adding the same colors in the same pattern around all the sides. Cut out with deckle-edged scissors when dry.

6 Change Colors and Repeat

On a smaller piece of glossy cardstock, repeat the process with the same colors, but this time add Peacock Blue, Apple Green and Blue Violet. Cover the whole sheet in the same manner focusing more on the newly added colors. Cut out with deckle-edged scissors.

7 Gild a Layer

Cut a piece of glossy cardstock with deckle-edged scissors to act as a frame for the smaller, watercolored background. Gild a ½" (1.3cm) border around all sides of the cardstock with a gold leafing pen. Let dry thoroughly.

8 Begin Building Layers

Layer the larger background onto a folded piece of white speckled cardstock with double-sided tape. Next center and add the gilded paper with double-sided tape.

9 Stamp and Gild Centerpiece

Stamp the shell stamp in Prussian Blue on a piece of glossy cardstock. Cut around the sides with deckle-edged scissors and gild edges with a gold leafing pen. Let dry thoroughly and then center mount with double-sided mounting tape to raise the image off the other layers.

ARCHITECTURALLY SPEAKING

Water play is one of my favorite art activities because I never get the same result twice. I always feel a certain amount of anticipation as I drop the colors onto the surface, and I love to watch them move and mingle after more water is added. Using highly pigmented watercolor or even diluted dye inks will produce the most vibrant results. Try different combinations of paint for a more exciting finished piece.

■ ■ ■ ■ MATERIALS LIST

- glossy white, yellow and purple cardstock

- waxy palette paper

- watercolors: Dr. Ph. Martin's Hydrus in Hansa Yellow Light, Cobalt Violet *(Salis International)*

- dye ink pad: Adirondack in Espresso *(Ranger)*

- 24-gauge gold wire

- 3" (7.5cm) foam brush

- spray bottle, filled with water

- round-nosed pliers

- toothbrush

- Da Vinci drawings background stamp *(JudiKins)*

Finished Size:
6" × 6" (15.2cm × 15.2cm)

1 Apply Colors to Palette

Dampen a 3" (7.5cm) foam brush and add three to four drops of Cobalt Violet. Spritz with a spray bottle to add more water and spread onto palette paper or other glossy surface.

2 Add Yellow to Palette

Add three to four Hansa Yellow Light drops to palette paper directly next to several of the larger Cobalt Violet pools of color. Some of the pools will start to mix and that is what you want.

3 Dip Into Palette

Place the glossy cardstock into the pooled color and lightly press down. Pull up carefully and turn over.

4 Splatter to Add More Texture

Use the remaining watercolor mixture to splatter onto the back ground with a toothbrush. This will add more texture to the negative space areas left after dipping, while still allowing the eye to rest.

5 Ink Background Stamp

Lay the Da Vinci stamp down and ink with Adirondack Espresso.

6 Stamp Over Background

Stamp Da Vinci stamp using even pressure onto watercolored background.

7 Add Wire and Mount

Cut two narrow strips of purple cardstock and attach to folded, yellow card. Cut a 5" (12.7cm) and a 3" (7.6cm) piece of wire. Use round-nosed pliers to coil and attach with double-sided tape to the yellow card. Affix watercolored cardstock on top with double-sided tape to finish.

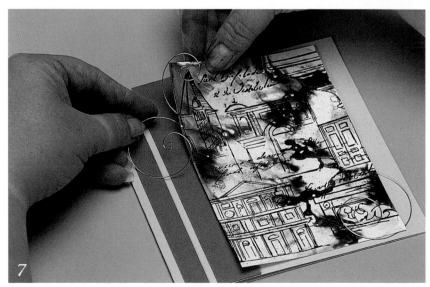

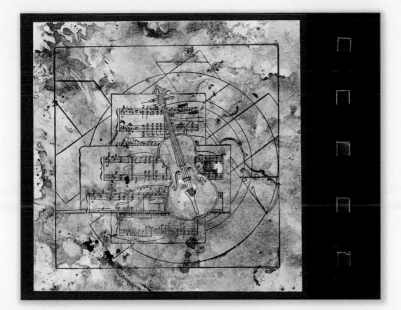

VARIATION:
CONCERTO

Create a mottled pattern with watercolor crayons in brown, black and yellow. Stamp with a musical collage stamp and a complementary ink onto the painted background. Mount onto dark brown cardstock, and add some antiqued larger square brads down one side. This card would work equally well for a male or female.

VARIATION:
WHIMSY

It is always interesting to follow the lines or patterns made by a watercolor print. For this print use watercolor crayons in blue and purple. Follow some of the lines made by the watercolor with fluid adhesive and then add micro beads. Add more detail with background stamps using Adirondack pads in colors similar to the crayons. Mount the card on dusty blue cardstock. Add charmed photo corners to dress it up a bit.

RESOURCES

STAMP COMPANIES

A Stamp in the Hand Co.
(310) 884-9700
www.astampinthehand.com

Above the Mark
(530) 666-6648
www.abovethemark.com

Alextamping
(888)-WE-DO-ART
www.alextamping.com

Art Impressions
(800) 393-2014
www.artimpressions.com

Eureka! Stamps
(800) 679-8740
www.eurekastamps.com

Great Impressions
Rubber Stamps, Inc.
(800) 373-5908
www.greatimpressionsstamps.com

Hampton Art Stamps
(800) 229-1019
www.hamptonart.com

Hero Arts
(800) 822-HERO
www.heroarts.com

Hot Potatoes
(615) 269-8002
www.hotpotatoes.com

Impression Obsession
(877) 259-0905
www.impression-obsession.com

JudiKins
www.judikins.com

Just For Fun Rubber Stamps
(727) 938-9898
www.jffstamps.com

Limited Edition, Inc.
(650) 594-4242
www.LimitedEditionRS.com

Magenta
www.magentastyle.com

Marks of Distinction
(773) 772-9300

Moe Wubba
(Time To Stamp)
(909) 845-9242
www.timetostamp.com

Moon Rose Art Stamps
(631) 549-0199
www.themoonroseartstamps.com

Fred B. Mullett
(206) 624-5723
www.fredbmullett.com

Paper Inspirations
(406) 756-9677
www.stampgallery.com

PostModern Design
PO Box 720416
Norman, OK 73070
(405) 321-3176

Printworks
(562) 906-1262
www.printworkscollection.com

PSX
(Duncan Enterprises)
(800) 438-6226
www.psxdesign.com

Rubber Poet
(800) 906-POET
www.rubberpoet.com

Rubber Tree Stamps
(413) 585-0875
www.rubbertreestamps.com

Stamp and Art Specialties
(636) 940-9900
www.stampart.net

Stamp Francisco
www.stampfrancisco.com
(877) 268-4869

Stamp Out Cute
Fresno, CA
(559) 323-7174

Stampers Anonymous
(The Creative Block)
www.stampersanonymous.com

Stampscapes
www.stampscapes.com

Toybox
(707) 431-7707
www.toyboxart.com

Treasure Cay
(727) 784-0880

Turtle Press Studio
(206) 706-3186
www.turtlearts.com

ZimPrints Rubber Stamps
www.zimprints.com

PAINTS & INKS

Clearsnap
888-448-4862
www.clearsnap.com
inks and applicators

Craf-T Products
(800) 530-3410
www.craf-tproducts.com
metallic rub-ons

Jacquard Products
(800) 442-0455
www.jacquardproducts.com
Lumiere, Pearl-Ex powders, Piñata inks

Krylon Products
(800) 797-3332
www.krylon.com
sealant, webbing, paint pens

Graphic Marker International
(818) 709-4512
www.artmarker.com
Studio II inks

Lyra
www.lyra.de
available through JudiKins
watercolor crayons

Plaid Enterprises, Inc.
800-842-4197
www.plaidonline.com
Glaze Vernis

Ranger Industries, Inc.
800-244-2211
www.rangerink.com
inks, ink pads

Salis International, Inc.
(800) 843-8293
www.docmartins.com
watercolors, other paints

Tsukineko, Inc.
(800) 769-6633
www.tsukineko.com
inks, ink pads

USArtQuest, Inc.
(800) 200-7848
www.usartquest.com
mica tiles, Jacquard products

EMBELLISHMENTS & FINISHING

Bonnie's Best
(404) 869-0081
www.stampsalad.com
button shank remover, paper trimmer, coil binder, other tools

McGill Incorporated
(800) 982-9884
www.mcgillinc.com
decorative punches

Lucky Squirrel
800-462-4912
www.luckysquirrel.com
shrink plastic

On The Surface
PO Box 8026
Wilmette, IL 60091
decorative fibers

Spectra Art Tissue
(Pacon Corporation)
Phone: 800-333-2545
sales@pacon.com
bleeding art tissue

Yasutomo
(800) 262-6454
available from JudiKins
Niji Waterbrush, gel pens

OTHER PRODUCTS

Creative Imaginations
(800) 942-6487
www.cigift.com
centering ruler

Dove Products
(800) 334-3683
www.dovebrushes.com
rubber squeegee

INDEX

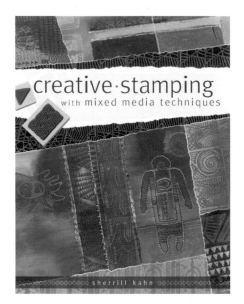